The Hostage

The Hostage

by

Brendan Behan

LONDON

METHUEN & CO LTD

36 ESSEX STREET · STRAND · WC2

First published in 1958

© *1958 by Theatre Workshop*

This play is fully protected by copyright. All inquiries concerning performing rights, professional or amateur, should be directed to Theatre Workshop, Theatre Royal, Stratford, London, E.15.

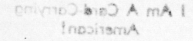

Catalogue Number 6138/U

Printed in Great Britain
by W. & J. Mackay & Co Ltd, Fair Row, Chatham

"The Hostage" *was first presented by Theatre Workshop at*
the Theatre Royal, Stratford, London, E.15, on 14th October,
1958, with the following cast:

PAT, *the caretaker of a lodging-house*	Howard Goorney
MEG DILLON	Avis Bunnage
MONSEWER, *the owner of the house*	Glynn Edwards
COLETTE	Leila Greenwood
BOBO	Annette Robertson
PRINCESS GRACE	Dudley Sutton
RIO RITA	Roy Barnett
MR. MULLEADY	Robin Chapman
MISS GILCHRIST, *a social worker*	Eileen Kennally
LESLIE, *a British soldier*	Murray Melvin
TERESA, *a country girl*	Celia Salkeld
I.R.A. OFFICER	James Booth
VOLUNTEER	Clive Barker

SAILORS, WHORES, POLICEMEN, ETC.

The play produced by Joan Littlewood

The Hostage was first presented by Theatre Workshop at the Theatre Royal, Stratford, London, E.15, on 14th October 1958, with the following cast:

PAT, the caretaker of a lodging-house	The 21st Century
MEG DILLON	Avis Bunnage
MONSEWER, the owner of the house	Glynn Edwards
COLETTE	Leila Greenwood
ROPO	Annette Robertson
PRINCESS GRACE	Dudley Sutton
ROPEEN	Roy Barnett
MR. MULLEADY	Brian Harpham
MISS GILCHRIST, a social worker	Eileen Kennally
LESLIE, a British soldier	Murray Melvin
TERESA, a country girl	Celia Salkeld
I.R.A. OFFICER	James Booth
VOLUNTEER	Clive Barker
& RUSSIAN SAILORS, SPANIARDS, ETC.	

The play produced by Joan Littlewood

ACT I

Curtain up.

Whole company dances an Irish Jig after two figures in which two whores and two queers have danced together; MULLEADY *is seen dancing with* MISS GILCHRIST.

1ST WHORE [*to* QUEERS]. Get off the stage, you dirty low things.

COLETTE. A decent whore can't get a shilling round here for the likes of you.

PRINCESS GRACE. To hell with you, and your friends in America. Come on, dear [*to* RIO], take no notice of them.

1ST WHORE. Go, get a mass said for yourself.

PRINCESS GRACE. What we need round here is a bit of tolerance.

Exit whores and queers.
A blast on bagpipes.

MEG. In the name of God, what's that?

PAT. It's only Monsewer practising his music. He has taken it into his head to play the Dead March for the boy in Belfast Jail when they hang him in the morning.

MEG. I wish he'd keep it in his head. Those bagpipes get on my nerves.

PAT. Get us a bottle of stout.

MEG. Get it yourself.

PAT. I'm not able.

MEG. Of course you're able.

PAT. Begod, the old leg's killing me tonight. I've a cruel pain where it used to be.

MEG. Get along with you, you old scow. Do you think they will hang him.

PAT. Who?

MEG. The boy in Belfast Jail.

PAT. There's no think about it. Tomorrow morning at the hour of eight, he'll hang as high as Killymanjaaro.

MEG. What the hell's that?

PAT. It's a noted mountain off the south coast of Switzerland. It would do you the world of no good to be hung as high as it, anyway.

MEG. Do you know what he said? "As a soldier of the Irish Republic, I will die smiling."

PAT. And who asked him to give himself the trouble?

MEG. He only did his duty as a member of the I.R.A.

PAT. Don't have me to use a coarse expression, you silly old bitch. This is nineteen-fifty-eight, and the days of the heroes is over this thirty-five years past. Long over, finished and done with. The I.R.A. and the War of Independence are as dead—as dead as the Charleston.

MEG. The old cause is never dead, till Ireland will be free from the centre to the sea. Hurrah for liberty, says the Shan Van Vocht.

PAT [sighs]. She's as bad as Monsewer. It's bad enough for that old idiot not to have a clock, but I declare to Jesus, I don't think he even has a calendar. And who has all the trouble of it? I have. He wants to have the new I.R.A., so called, in this place now. "Prepare a room for them," no less. Bad enough running this place as a speak-easy and a brockel—

MEG. A what?

PAT. A brockel—that's English for a whorehouse.

MEG. I will be thankful to you to keep that kind of talk about whorehouses to yourself. I'm no whore for one!

PAT. Why? Are you after losing your union card?

MEG. Well, if I'm a whore itself, you don't mind taking the best part of my money. So you're nothing but a ponce.

PAT. Well, I'm saving up to be one! [*Mutters.*] And a good while that'll take with the money you earn.

MEG. Oh it will.

PAT. Yes.

MEG. Well, you know what you can do.

They sit with their backs to each other.

PAT. You ought to know better than to abuse me, a poor crippled man that lost his leg on the field of slaughter, three miles outside the town of Mullingar. And how do you think any of us could keep the house going on what I get from Monsewer? And who would look after him, in England or Ireland, if I didn't? I stick by him, because we were soldiers of Ireland in the old days: can I sing my old song to him?

MEG. I suppose so.

PAT [*sings*]:

> On the eighteenth day of November,
> Just outside the town of Macroom,
> The 'Tans in their big Crossley tenders,
> Came roaring along to their doom,
> But the boys of the column were waiting
> With hand grenades primed on the spot,
> And the Irish Republican Army
> Made quit of the whole bleeding lot.

MEG. You're always singing about them ould times, and the five glorious years, and still you sneer and jeer at the boys nowadays. What's the difference?

PAT. The H-Bomb. I'm nervous of it. It's such a big bomb it's after making me scared of little bombs. The I.R.A. is out of date and so is the R.A.F. So is the Swiss Guard and the Foreign Legion, the Red Army, the United States Marines, the Free State Army.

MEG. And the Civic Guards?

PAT. The Coldstream Guards, the Scots Guards, the Welsh Guards, the Grenadier Guards—

The sound of the pipes again. This time they are playing "O'Donnell Aboo".

MEG. Here is Monsewer, now.

PAT [*puts his two hands over his ears*]. I hear him. Jasus, amn't I deaf with him?

Enter MONSEWER. He is a tall man, with a large white moustache. He is wearing a kilt, and carries his pipes with a noble air. He blows a last long note on the pipes.

MONSEWER. Good day to you.

PAT [*coming to attention like an old soldier*]. Commandant-General!

MONSEWER [*salutes*]. As you were. [*He nods towards* MEG.)

PAT [*to* MEG]. Go out there and be sweeping the stairs.

[MEG *takes the hint and goes out.*]

Well, the room is cleaned out and prepared as you see.

MONSEWER. Good, good. The troops will be coming quite soon.

PAT [*aside*]. The troops. Good God. [*To* MONSEWER.] How many of them are expected, then.

MONSEWER. There will be the two guards and the prisoner.

PAT. The prisoner?

MONSEWER. Yes. Yes, we only have the one at the moment, but it's a good beginning.

PAT. Yes, indeed, as the Scotchman says, "Many a mickle makes a muckle."

MONSEWER. And as we Irish say, "It was one after another they built the castles—Iss in yeeg a kale-ah shah togeock nuh cashlawn."

PAT. That's Irish. Isn't it great for them that has an Oxford University education. God help me, I'm only a poor ignorant Dublin man. I wouldn't understand a word of it. The prisoner you were talking about, sir?

MONSEWER. Yes. An English soldier they captured in Armagh last night. One only. But that's only the beginning. Before long we'll have scores of them.

PAT [aside]. I hope to God he's not going to bring them all here.

MONSEWER. What's that?

PAT [in a louder tone]. It's a great thing, I say, that the boys are out again.

MONSEWER. It's wonderful. Carry on. [Exit.]

MEG. He's a decent old skin, even if he has got a slate loose.

PAT. Did you hear that? I thought it was bad enough making a sort of I.R.A. barracks out of this place, but it's worse than that. Monsewer is going to make a glasshouse out of it. A kind of private Shepton Mallet of his own.

MEG. We should be proud to help the men that are fighting for Ireland. Especially that poor boy to be hanged in Belfast Jail tomorrow morning.

PAT. Why are you getting so upset over Ireland? Where the hell were you in nineteen-sixteen when the real fighting was going on?

MEG. I wasn't born.

PAT [*throws up his two hands*]. You're full of excuses! Where the hell were they when we had to go out and capture our own stuff off of the British Army?

MEG. You told me that you bought it off the Tommies in the pub. You said yourself you got a revolver, two hundred rounds of ammunition, and a pair of jodhpurs off a colonel's batman for two pints of Bass and fifty Woodbines.

PAT. I shouldn't have given him anything. But I was sorry for him.

MEG. Why?

PAT. He was engaged to my sister-in-law.

There is a sound of a row upstairs. MR. MULLEADY *rushes down.*

MR. MULLEADY. Oh! Mr. Pat, something terrible is happening!

PAT. What's going on?

COLETTE [*yelling*]. Get out, you dirty foreign bastard.

SAILOR *protests in Polish.*

Do you know what he is? A Pole, he is. Off one of the Polish coal boats that's just in. Pat, will you give us a hand? Mr. Mulleady told me just now, he's a Pole, he is.

PAT. What's wrong with that? Is he dirty or something?

MR. MULLEADY. Worse than that, Mr. Pat. He's a communist, that's what's wrong with it, my friend. [MEG *moves away from him.*]

COLETTE. Go on out.

PAT. What's got into you?

MEG. Pat, it's against my religion, I tell you, to have to do with the likes of him.

MR. MULLEADY. That's what I told her.

PAT. Ah, sure you have to pick up trade where you can get it these days.

MR. MULLEADY. Mr. Pat, I'm surprised at you saying a thing like that.

COLETTE. Will you throw him out of here?

PAT. The only reason I know for throwing a man out is when he has no money to pay.

MEG. Has he got any?

POLE. Da?

PAT. I'll find out. Got any gelt? Dollars? Pound notes? Money?

POLE. Oh da, da.

Empties pockets, which have many notes in them. Offers them to COLETTE.

MEG. Do you see the wad he has on him?

COLETTE *crosses herself then takes some*. MR. MULLEADY *picks one up.*

COLETTE. Come on.

MEG. Pound notes is the best religion in the world.

PAT. And the best politics.

MONSEWER *enters—he speaks in Irish to the* POLE, *who responds in* POLISH.

MONSEWER. Carry on, my dear. Ireland needs the work of women as well, you know. [*Exit.*]

COLETTE. I know that, Monsewer. And a bed in heaven to you.

PAT *indicates that the* POLE *should go up with* COLETTE.

POLE. Spasiba. [*Exeunt* POLE *and* COLETTE.]

PAT. And the same to you.

MR. MULLEADY. I'm sorry Mrs. M.—I mean about the Pole. I felt that as a God-fearing man I could shut my eyes no longer.

PAT. It's a pity you don't close them indefinitely.

MEG. Ah, get along with you. Anybody would think you was doing God a good turn speaking well of him.

MR. MULLEADY. Oh, and another thing—about my laundry, Miss Meg. It was due back three days ago. I have to go to one of my committees this evening and I haven't a shirt to my name.

PAT. It walked back.

MEG. Go and ask the Prisoners Aid Society to help you.

MR. MULLEADY. You know very well that that is the committee on which I serve.

MEG. Well, go and wash one.

MR. MULLEADY. You know I can't . . .

MEG. Get going, or I'll ask you for the money you owe me.

MR. MULLEADY. Please don't bring all that up again. You know that at the end of the month . . .

MEG. Are you going . . . [MR. MULLEADY goes.] Fine thing to be letting rooms to every class of gouger and bowsey in the city.

PAT. Dirty thieves and whores the lot of them. Still, their money is clean enough.

MEG. It's not the whores I mind, it's the likes of that old whited sepulchre. That I don't like.

PAT. You don't mean Monsewer?

MEG. No I don't, I mean that old Mulleady geezer, though that old Monsewer is bad enough, giving out about the Republic and living in a brockel.

PAT. He doesn't know a thing about that; he thinks it's the War of Independence that's still going on.

MEG. He doesn't.

PAT. He does. He thinks all the people that come here are all Gaels and Republicans and patriots on the run.

MEG. The old idiot. He's here again.

MONSEWER. Patrick.

PAT. Commandant-General.

MONSEWER. As you were.

PAT. Thank you, Monsewer.

MONSEWER. I trust we may rely on the lads in the billet if anything should go wrong.

PAT. We may put our lives in their hands, Monsewer.

MEG. God help us.

MONSEWER. That's all I wanted to know. There seemed to be a bit of rumpus in here a minute ago.

PAT. Someone dropped something, sir.

MONSEWER. Bound to be a bit restless, I suppose, on a night like this.

PAT. It's the strain of battle, Commandant.

MONSEWER. Carry on. You've plenty of fodder in.

PAT. For the horses, Commandant?

MONSEWER. For the men, for the men.

PAT. Oh yes—I mean Monsewer—it's funny how I still can't get used to the foreign title. Even after all these years. I mean Monsewer.

MONSEWER. French for Mister, you know, Patrick.

PAT. I never did understand how you came by it, Commandant.

MONSEWER. I wanted no truck with the English titles, my man; as you know, for some time I refused to use their language altogether.

PAT. Yes indeed, sir. When Monsewer came here, Meg, he wouldn't talk anything but Irish.

MEG. Most people wouldn't know what he was saying, surely.

PAT. They did not. When he went on a tram car or a bus he had to have an interpreter with him so as the conductor would know where he wanted to get off.

MEG. Ah, the poor man.

MONSEWER. Mister and missus are English forms of address.

MEG. I know the Irish for missus, Monsewer. It's Ban, isn't it? Now if you'd said that, Monsewer, I'd have been with you.

MONSEWER. Ban in the English means woman. So if your husband's name was Murphy, you'd be called Ban Murphy, Murphy's woman. Not really in the best of taste, you know.

PAT. Do you see now, Meg? [*Aside to* MEG.] These high-up old ones couldn't stick that at all, it was a bit too Irish that was, so they called themselves "madame".

MONSEWER. Madame, a fitting mode of address for a daughter of Ireland. Oh, by the by, Patrick—a patriot of ours called Pigseye has just done six months for the cause. He's to billet here at our expense till the end of his days.

PAT. Yes, sir.

MONSEWER. Carry on. [*He goes.*]

PAT. The patriot Pigseye has just done six months for robbery with violence.

MEG. Don't talk to me about Pigseye. He's as mean as the grave. He knocked off a hundred gross of nylons from the Haute Couture warehouse and not one did he offer to a girl in the street. No Bejasus, not even to the one-legged girl in No. 8.

PAT. I'll get the rent off him or he'll reach the end of his days sooner than he expects.

MEG. Still, Monsewer meant well.

PAT. He's not a bad old skin, for an Englishman.

MEG. You what?

PAT. I said for an Englishman.

MEG. An Englishman, and him going round in his kilt playing his big Gaelic pipes all day.

PAT. He was born an Englishman and remained one for years. His father was a bishop.

MEG. His father was a bishop. I'm not sitting here listening to that class of immoral talk. His father a bishop indeed.

PAT [*impatiently*]. He was a Protestant bishop.

MEG. Ah well, of course it's different with them, isn't it?

PAT. Monsewer went to one of these big colleges in England, and he slept in one room with the King of England's son.

MEG. It wouldn't surprise me if he slept in one bed with him, his father being a bishop.

PAT. He had riches and every class of comfort you could wish for, till he found out he was an Irishman.

MEG. Aren't you after telling me he was an Englishman?

PAT. He was an Anglo-Irishman.

MEG. In the blessed name of God, what's that?

PAT. A Protestant with a horse.

MEG. And what do they do when they're out?

PAT. Well, an Anglo-Irishman only works at riding horses, you know, and drinking whisky, or reading double-meaning books in Irish at Trinity College.

MEG. I'm with you now; he wasn't born one, he became one.

H.–B

PAT. He didn't become one—he was one—on his mother's side, and as he didn't like his father much he went with his mother's people—he became an Irishman.

MEG. How did he do that?

PAT. Well, there's not all that much difference. He started going to the Irish classes in the Gaelic League in Red Lion Passage and wearing a kilt and playing Gaelic football on Blackheath, but then he threw the hammer after the hatchet and acted like a true Irishman here.

MEG. He came over to live in Ireland.

PAT. He fought for Ireland. Where's that girl with me cigarettes?

MEG. I can't think where she's got to. She's been gone an hour now.

PAT. Well, give me a pint of stout.

MEG. I will an' all, and myself one too.

PAT. He came over to die for Ireland.

MEG. Sure, many's the time you've been telling me stories about the times you was active; Monsewer on the back of his white horse at the head of his regiment, the cross of Christ held high in his right hand like Brian Boru in the battle of Clontarf leading his men to war and glory. Didn't you tell me about the time he was a corporal down at Cork?

PAT. He was not a corporal, but a general.

MEG. What difference is it, corporal, general or admiral? I knew he was some sort of ral.

PAT. As a matter of fact, he was an old idiot.

MEG. He can't be such an idiot or they wouldn't be sending fellows in from the I.R.A. today, officers and all.

PAT. What are you talking about?

MEG. I mean that young fellow that was in here the other day.

PAT. How did you know he was an officer?

MEG. Sure they wouldn't send an ordinary Joe Soap to see Monsewer, would they? In any case, you don't think I'm such a fool as not to know what's cooking here, do you? I've got eyes in my head.

PAT. Keep your mouth shut and don't be comparing that little rat of a fellow that was in here yesterday to a soldier like Monsewer and myself.

MEG. Even if he is half mad?

PAT. He wasn't half mad the first time I saw him, nor a quarter mad, God bless him.

MEG. Amen, amen. What drove him half mad then?

PAT. The treaty.

MEG. What?

PAT. The treaty. Some of our leaders made an agreement to have no more fighting with England.

MEG. The traitors.

PAT. Sure, they sold the six counties and Irishmen were forced to swear an oath to the British Crown.

MEG. I don't know about the six counties, but I shouldn't think the swearing would come so hard on you.

PAT. Five years' hard fighting—nobody knows what it was like. Heavy and many is the good man was killed—and we had victory at last—till they signed that Curse of God Treaty in London.

MEG. Whatever made them do it?

PAT. Well, Lloyd George and Birkenhead made a fool of Michael Collins and he signed it.

MEG. He should have been shot.

PAT. He was.

MEG. Ah, the poor man.

PAT. He was a great soldier and fought well for the old cause all the same for five long years. We used to call him the Laughing Boy. We'll sing my song for him—

'Twas on an August morning, all in the morning hours,
I went to take the warming air all in the month of flowers,
And there I saw a maiden and heard her mournful cry,
Oh what will mend my broken heart, I've lost my laughing boy.

So strong, so wide and brave he was, I'll mourn his loss too sore
When thinking that we'll hear the laugh or springing step no more,
Ah, curse the time, and sad the loss my heart to crucify
That an Irish son, with a rebel gun, shot down my laughing boy.

Oh had he died by Pearse's side or in the G.P.O.
Killed by an English bullet from the rifle of the foe
Or forcibly fed while Ashe lay dead in the dungeons of Mountjoy,
I'd have cried with pride at the way he died, my own dear laughing boy.

My princely love, can ageless love do more than tell to you
Go raibh mile maith Agath, for all you tried to do.
For all you did and would have done, my enemies to destroy,
I'll praise your name and guard your fame, my own dear laughing boy.

PAT [*sighing*]. Ah sure, it's a great story!

MEG. It's better than the show that used to be on the television below in Tom English's Eagle Bar, "This is Your Life".

PAT. It was not the end of the story. Some of us didn't accept the treaty. We went out fighting again—and we were beat. But Monsewer was loyal to the old cause and I was loyal to Monsewer. So when the fighting was done we came back together to this old house.

MEG. This dirty old hole.

PAT. Yes, and a good hole it was for many a decent man on the run for twenty years after that.

MEG. Who the hell was still running twenty years after that?

PAT. All true Republicans who wouldn't accept the treaty. Cosgrave was hunting the Republicans, so they put de Valera in and he started hunting them too.

MEG. I see—says the blind man. Well carry on with the coffin, the corpse can walk.

PAT. In the end it was no paying game—hiding hunted Republicans, so we had to take in all sorts of scruffy lumpers to make the place pay. This noble old house which housed so many heroes was turned into a knocking shop. Still, I had you to help me.

MEG [in tears]. Oh you lousy bastard. The curse of God meet and melt you and your rotten lousy leg. You had me to help you, indeed. If I'm a whore itself, sure I'm a true patriot.

PAT. Ah sure and I know that, my dear. Now listen to me— sure you didn't think it was you I was talking about. Aren't we man and wife . . . nearly?

MEG. Yes, Pat, we are—well, nearly.

PAT. Sure I wasn't referring to you or meaning you at all, alana. I was talking about Ropeen and Colette, that pair of brasses, and the Mouse, Pigseye and Bobo. Nobody could deny that they're a pack of whores and thieves.

MEG. No indeed, that Colette anyway after what she done to the poor old Civil Servant out of the Ministry of . . .

PAT [*interrupting*]. Never mind that now.

MEG. Ah well now, Pat, it was no joke, and the poor old man on his knees at the bedside saying his prayers, to go robbing his money and him wearing nothing but his night-shirt, in the presence of Almighty God so to speak.

PAT. No, sure you couldn't blame me, darling, for anything I would call the like of her.

MEG. Certainly not I couldn't. Here's Princess Grace coming down now.

PAT. For Jasus' sake don't let on to any of them scruffs for what you know will be happening here tonight.

MEG. Mum's the word.

PRINCESS GRACE *enters with* RIO RITA.

PRINCESS GRACE. Isn't he marvellous?

PAT. Have you your rent?

PRINCESS GRACE. Of course, dear. I've never been at a loss yet, have I? You'll never guess how I got it this time. I hadn't been out five—

PAT. Never mind that now. Give me it. It's all one to me how you got it once you have it.

PRINCESS GRACE. There you are, Judas.

PAT. Thanks. [*Takes a book from his pocket.*] Now what's this your name is? I can't put down Princess Grace.

PRINCESS GRACE. No dear, that's only my name in religion.

MEG. Don't be giving out that talk about religion now.

PRINCESS GRACE. He's lovely, isn't he?

PAT. Here we are, week ending the twenty-second, received with thanks from John L. Sullivan.

PRINCESS GRACE [*simpering*]. That was my maiden name, darling. Oh, by the way, I've something to tell you. About that Mr. Mulleady. I think it's disgraceful. It certainly makes very little of you, Meg, and all the other girls in the house.

MEG. What are you talking about?

PRINCESS GRACE. It's about the fifth floor back, you know, Mr. Mulleady.

MEG. What about him?

PRINCESS GRACE. I wouldn't think much of myself if people brought strange women into the house anyway, and me a working girl.

MEG. What are you talking about.

PRINCESS GRACE. A strange woman, dear, not a woman of the house, an outsider. Three-quarters of an hour she's been in there and the noises—

PAT. What sort of a woman?

PRINCESS GRACE. A female woman.

MEG. The dirty, low degenerate old maniac, what does he take this house for? [*Calling*.] Mr. Mulleady!

    MISS GILCHRIST *is heard singing*.

MEG. Mr. Mulleady!

MR. MULLEADY [*calling*]. Is that you, Mrs. M.?

MEG. Is it me? Who do you think it is? Come down to hell out of there at once, and bring that shameless bitch along with you.

PRINCESS GRACE [*to* PAT]. Here he comes with his airs and graces.

MR. MULLEADY. Did you call me, Mrs. M. dear? And what is it you'll be wanting?

MEG. If Mulleady is your name, I called you. And I called that low whore you have up in your room as well. I didn't call her by her name, because I don't know what it is, if she has one at all. [*Calls again.*] Come down here, you whore, whoever you are.

MR. MULLEADY. My dear Mrs. M., I beg of you, she might hear you.

MEG. Who's she when she's at home? What's she got that I haven't got, I'd like to know?

MR. MULLEADY. She is a lady.

MEG. More shame to her. And don't call me your dear Mrs. M. again nor your cheap Mrs. K. either.

MR. MULLEADY. I wouldn't dream of such a thing, nor would I dream of bringing—

MEG. Dream of what?

MR. MULLEADY. A—a—the type you mention into this house.

PAT. It'd only be coals to Newcastle.

MEG. Now, Mr. Mulleady, Mr. Mulleady sir, don't you know you could have got anything like that here? I'm surprised at you, so I am. God knows I've stood by you through thick and thin even when that man there was wanting to cast you out into the streets for the low-down dirty old lag that you are.

They run round room.

MR. MULLEADY. Mrs. M., must we bring that up? We are trying to forget the painful past.

MEG. Ran away with the Church funds, he did.

MR. MULLEADY. Mrs. M., please.

MEG. And that's not the worst of it.

MR. MULLEADY. Not in front of strangers, I beg of you.

PRINCESS GRACE. And he told me he was something in the city.

MR. MULLEADY. Be quiet. You—you wasp.

PRINCESS GRACE. Oh buzz.

MR. MULLEADY. Go away. Mrs. M., please say no more. I'm sorry, please—

MEG. Call down that brasstitute.

MR. MULLEADY. She's—

MEG. Get her down out of that.

MR. MULLEADY [calls]. Miss Gilchrist!

MISS GILCHRIST is singing.

MEG. Louder.

MR. MULLEADY. Miss Gilchrist!

MISS GILCHRIST. Yes, Mr. Mulleady.

MR. MULLEADY. Will you come down a minute, please?

MISS GILCHRIST. I haven't finished the first novena, Mr. Mulleady.

MEG. Never mind the—

MR. MULLEADY. Mrs. Meg. Please, I'll get her down. To-morrow is another day, Miss Gilchrist. If you'll put on your hat we'll go out and take the air.

MEG. "Put on her hat." I'll give her hat.

A humming is heard.

MISS GILCHRIST. I'm coming. [She descends.] Well, who are all those good people?

MR. MULLEADY. That's er—this is er—she's—Mrs. Meg, Miss Gilchrist, Miss Gil—

MEG. Gilchrist! In the name of Christ, what kind of a name is Gilchrist?

MISS GILCHRIST. It is an old Irish name. In its original form "Giolla Christ", the servant or gilly of Christ.

MEG. You're a quare ould gilly of Christ, you whore.

MISS GILCHRIST. I take insults in the name of our insulted Saviour.

MEG. You take anything you can get, like a good many more. You've been three hours up in Mr. Mulleady's room.

MR. MULLEADY. A quarter of an hour, Mrs. M.

MEG. Shut up.

MISS GILCHRIST. We were speaking of our souls.

> MR. MULLEADY *and* MISS GILCHRIST *sing—"Our Souls, Our Souls."*

MEG. You can leave his soul alone, whatever about your own soul, you bloody bitch. And take yourself out of here, before I'm dug out of you.

MISS GILCHRIST. I will give you my prayers.

MEG. You can shove 'em up in your cathedral.

MISS GILCHRIST. I forgive you. You are a poor sinful person.

MEG. And you're a half-time whore.

PAT. Compliments pass when the quality meet.

MISS GILCHRIST. Eustace.

> *Everyone looks round sharply.*

MR. MULLEADY. Yes—er—Miss Gilchrist.

MISS GILCHRIST. Come away. This is Sodom and Gomorrah.

> MEG *grabs him.*

MR. MULLEADY. I can't, Miss Gilchrist. I haven't paid my rent.

MISS GILCHRIST. I will pray for you, Eustace; my umbrella, please.

MR. MULLEADY. Will you come back, Miss Gilchrist?

MISS GILCHRIST. Our Lord will give me strength. [*To* PRINCESS GRACE.] God go with you. [*She goes.*]

MR. MULLEADY [*after her*]. Evangelina! [*She turns, salutes and goes.*]

PAT. Ships that pass in the night.

MEG. Did you ever see anything like it in your life? And now are you going to ask for an explanation, or am I?

PAT. Leave me out of it. You brought him here in the first place.

MEG. So I did, God help me. And you take your face out of here, you simpering little get.

MR. MULLEADY *makes to go.*

Not you, him.

PRINCESS GRACE. Who told you what was going on in the first place? There's gratitude. I always knew what he was! The old eyebox!

MR. MULLEADY. Informer!

PRINCESS GRACE [*going*]. Oh spit!

MR. MULLEADY. Layabout.

PRINCESS GRACE. Thief! [*To audience.*] I think they're all a load of beasts. [*Goes.*]

MEG. Well?

MR. MULLEADY. All this fuss over nothing. Poor Miss G. came to talk to me about religion.

MEG. That kind is the worst kind. You can take it from me.

PAT. From one who knows.

MR. MULLEADY. I won't be restrained like this, I tell you. I must be free of your remonstrances, Mrs. M. You don't seem aware of my antecedents, my second cousin was a Kilkenny from Kilcock.

MEG. I'll cock you— Take this broom and sweep out your room, you whoremaster.

MR. MULLEADY. I will not be treated this way. [*Goes.*]

MEG [*chasing him*]. Take that! And go and sweep your room.

PAT. If the performance is over I'd like a cigarette.

MEG. I sent the skivvy out for them an hour ago. God knows where she's got to on the way. Have a Gollywog.

PAT. What in Jasus' name is that?

MEG. It's a French cigarette. I got them off that young attaché case at the French Embassy—the one that thinks all Irishwomen are his mother.

PAT. I don't like the look of them. I'll wait for me twenty Afton. Meanwhile I'll sing that famous old song, "The Hound that Caught the Pubic Hare".

MEG. You're always announcing these songs, but you never sing them.

PAT. Well, there is one I sing sometimes.

PAT [*sings*].

> There's no place on earth like the world
> Just between you and me
> There's no place on earth like the world
> Acushla, astore and machree.

TERESA *runs in.*

PAT. Musha, a hundred thousand welcomes to you, my colleen.

TERESA [*out of breath*]. Your cigarettes, sir. . . .

MEG. You were a long time gone for them. Were you lost in the place?

TERESA. I was, nearly. Shall I get on with the beds, Meg?

MEG. Yes, you can.

PAT. There's no sir but Monsewer in this house, my girl.

TERESA. Yes, sir.

PAT. Call me Pat.

TERESA. Pat, sir— Oh, by the way, there's a man outside.

MEG. Is he coming in?

TERESA. Well, he's just looking.

PAT. Is he a policeman?

TERESA. Oh no, sir, he looks respectable.

PAT [*going in to look*]. Where is he now?

TERESA. He's there, sir Pat.

> The I.R.A. MAN *is gazing up at the street.*

PAT. I can't see without my glasses. Has he a trench coat and a badge?

TERESA. He has, sir, how did you know?

MEG. He's a fortune teller.

TERESA. The badge says he only speaks Irish.

PAT. Begod, then him and me would have to use the deaf and dumb language, for the only bit of Irish I can say would get us both prosecuted. That badge makes me think he's an officer.

MEG. An officer?

TERESA. He has another to say he doesn't drink.

PAT. That makes him a higher officer.

MEG. Begod, keep him out of here.

PAT. He'll come in, in his own good time. Now, Teresa girl, you haven't been here long but you can be trusted to keep your mouth shut?

TERESA. Oh yes, I can, sir.

PAT. We'll be having someone staying here; you'll bring him his meals. Now if you don't tell a living sinner about it, you can stay here for the rest of your life.

MEG. Well, till she's married anyway.

TERESA. Oh thank you, sir, indeed I'm very happy here.

PAT. You're welcome!

TERESA. And I hope you'll be satisfied with my work.

PAT. I'll be satisfied if you'll do a bit more laughing and not be so serious.

TERESA. I've always been a very serious girl.

Sings "Open the Door Softly".

Open the door softly,
Shut it—keep out the draught,
For years and years, I've shed millions of tears,
And never but once have I laughed.

'Twas the time the holy picture fell,
And knocked my old granny cold,
While she knitted and sang an old Irish song,
'Twas by traitors poor Ulster was sold.

So open the window softly,
For Jaysus' sake hang the latch,
Come in and lie down and afterwards,
You can ask me what's the catch.

Before these foreign-born bastards, dear,
See you don't let yourself down.
We'll be the Lion and Unicorn,
My Rose unto your Crown.

MEG. Hasn't she got a nice voice, Pat?

PAT. Ah! that makes a nice picture; do you know what you look like, Meg?

MEG. Yes, a whore with a heart of gold; at least, that's what you'd say if you were drunk enough!

    Enter THE OFFICER.
    He reads list of defects—

OFFICER. House part of main block in street separated from rest by half-ruined house. Two exit doors, access to the roof by trap door.

PAT. All correct, sir.

OFFICER. Six flights of stairs including steps to basement, at present blocked by rubbish. Will you have that cleared, please?

PAT. Impossible, sir, there's no rubbish there. [*Ad lib. list of articles in cellar.*]

OFFICER. The cellar must be cleared. Will you check that, please? Who are these women? [*Hands him paper. Indicates that women must go. They leave.*]

PAT. Wait till I get me glasses. [*He fishes out a large monocle.*]

OFFICER [*striding up and down*]. You have food in sufficient for one day?

PAT. We have, sir; we always take care of the scoff.

OFFICER. May I see the toilet arrangements?

PAT. This way, sir. Mind your head as you go in.

    THE OFFICER *returns almost immediately and walks to the window.*

MONSEWER [*putting his head around door*]. Are you the fellow from H.Q.? Righteo. Carry on.

OFFICER. Who the hell was that?

PAT. My mother.

OFFICER. Can we be serious?

PAT. Sir!

OFFICER. Sign that paper if the facts are correct.

PAT. All correct, sir.

OFFICER. Now your rent books, please, or a list of the tenants.

PAT. I can give you that easy. There's Bobo, Ropeen, Colette, the Mouse, Pigseye, Mulleady, Princess Grace, Rio Rita, Meg, the new girl, and myself.

OFFICER [PAT *fetches his note-book*]. I'll tell you the truth, if it was my doings there'd be no such thing as us coming here. I'd have nothing to do with the place, and the bad reputation it has all over the city.

PAT. Isn't it good enough for your prisoner?

OFFICER. It's not good enough for the Irish Republican Army.

PAT. Isn't it now?

OFFICER. Patrick Pearse said "To serve a cause which is splendid and holy, men must themselves be splendid and holy."

PAT. Are you splendid, or just holy? Haven't I seen you somewhere before? It couldn't be you that was after coming here one Saturday night . . .

OFFICER. It could not.

PAT. It could have been your brother, for he was the spitting image of you.

OFFICER. If any of us were caught here now or at any time, it's shamed before the world we'd be. Still, I see their reasons for choosing it too.

PAT. The place is so hot, it's cold.

OFFICER. The police wouldn't believe we'd touch it.

PAT. If we're all caught here, it's not the opinion of the world or the police will be upsetting us, but the opinion of the Military Court. But then I suppose it's all the same to you; you'll be a hero, will you not?

OFFICER. I hope that I could never betray my trust.

PAT. Ah yes, of course, you've not yet been in Mountjoy or the Curragh glasshouse.

OFFICER. I have not.

PAT. That's easily seen in you.

OFFICER. I assure you, my friend, I'm not afraid of Red-caps.

PAT. Take it from me, they're not the worst [*to audience*] though they're bastards anywhere and everywhere. No, your real trouble when you go to prison as a patriot, do you know what it will be?

OFFICER. The loss of liberty.

PAT. No, the other Irish patriots, in along with you. Which branch of the I.R.A. are you in?

OFFICER. There is only one branch of the Irish Republican Army.

PAT. I was in the I.R.A. in 1916, and in 1925 H.Q. sent me from Dublin to the County Kerry because the agricultural labourers were after taking over five thousand acres of an estate from Lord Trales. They had it all divided very nice and fair among themselves, and were ploughing and planting in great style. G.H.Q. gave orders that they were to get off the land, that the social question would be settled when we got the thirty-county Republic. The Kerrymen said they weren't greedy like. They didn't want the whole thirty-two counties to begin with, and their five thousand acres would do them for a start.

OFFICER. Those men were wrong on the social question.

H.–C

PAT. Faith and I don't think it was questions they were interested in, at all, but answers. Anyway I agreed with them, and stopped there for six months training the local unit to take on the I.R.A., the Free State Army, aye, or the British Navy if it had come to it.

OFFICER. That was mutiny.

PAT. I know. When I came back to Dublin, I was court-martialled in my absence and sentenced to death in my absence, so I said they could shoot me in my absence. [*Pause.*]

OFFICER. Silence!

PAT. Sir!

OFFICER. I was sent here to do certain business. I would like to conclude that business.

PAT. Let us proceed, shall we, sir? When may we expect the prisoner?

OFFICER. Today.

PAT. What time?

OFFICER. Between nine and twelve.

PAT. Where is he now?

OFFICER. We haven't got him yet.

PAT. You haven't got a prisoner? Are you going down to Woolworths to buy one then?

OFFICER. I have no business telling you any more than has already been communicated to you.

PAT. Sure, I know that.

OFFICER. The arrangements are made for his reception. I will be here.

PAT. Well, the usual terms, rent in advance, please.

OFFICER. Is it looking for money you are?

PAT. What else? We're not a charity. Rent in advance.

OFFICER. I might have known what to expect. I know your reputation.

PAT. How did you hear of our little convent?

OFFICER. I do social work for the St. Vincent de Paul Society.

PAT. I always thought they were all ex-policemen. In the old days we wouldn't go near them.

OFFICER. In the old days there were Communists in the I.R.A.

PAT. There were, faith, and plenty of them. What of it!

OFFICER. The man that is most loyal to his faith is the one that will prove most loyal to the cause.

PAT. Have you your initials mixed up? Is it the F.B.I. or the I.R.A. that you are in?

OFFICER. If I didn't know that you were out in 1916 I'd think you were highly suspect.

PAT. Sir?

OFFICER. Well, at least you can't be an informer.

PAT. Ah, you're a shocking decent person. Could you give me a testimonial I could use in my election address if I wanted to get into the corporation? The rent, please!

OFFICER. I haven't got it on me.

PAT. Isn't it better for yourself that you pay me the rent? Then if we're caught you can disown me—say I only did it for money.

OFFICER. Thinking of your own skin.

PAT. I was thinking of the movement's great reputation. Four pounds, please.

OFFICER. I tell you I haven't got it on me.

PAT. Then get it. If you haven't got it by the time your man arrives, I'll throw the lot of you, prisoner and escort, out by the scruff of the neck into the street.

OFFICER [*going to his hidden gun*]. I wouldn't be too sure about that.

MEG [*at the door*]. Can we come in now, Pat?

PAT. What do you want?

MEG. We want to put the sheets on the bed.

OFFICER. Who are these women?

PAT. Sure it's only Meg and Teresa. Come in.

MEG *and* TERESA *make the bed.*

OFFICER [*sotto voce*]. Tell them to be quick about it.

PRINCESS GRACE [*calling as he comes down the stairs*]. Pat—Mr. Pat.

PAT. What is it?

PRINCESS GRACE. I've got the news on my portable—listen—it's still going on.

MEG. What's on? We don't want to hear any of your bloody old jazz screeching, we hear enough of that all day coming from your room.

PRINCESS GRACE. No, it's the news about that lovely young man, you know the one that they're going to be hanging in Belfast.

EVERYBODY. They're going to hang him? They really are?

PRINCESS GRACE. Quiet everybody, it's still on.

PAT. I can't make out a word it says on that thing.

MR. MULLEADY *has entered behind* PRINCESS GRACE.

PRINCESS GRACE *is listening to the radio*, MR. MULLEADY *is explaining what the news item said. While it continues* MR. MULLEADY *speaks.*

MR. MULLEADY. A young man, eighteen years of age—it was made on behalf of the Government of Northern Ireland.

PRINCESS GRACE. Shhhhh.

MR. MULLEADY. It's to be eight o'clock tomorrow morning. No reprieve. The Lord Lieutenant—final, I'm afraid.

PRINCESS GRACE. Shhhhh. I can't get it now. Eight o'clock tomorrow morning as arranged.

PAT. Turn the bloody thing off.

MEG. God help us all.

TERESA. The poor boy.

PRINCESS GRACE. Eight o'clock in the morning—think of it.

MEG. Ah sure, they might have mercy on him yet. Eighteen years of age—the poor boy.

OFFICER. Irishmen have been hanged by the Englishmen at eighteen years of age before this. Not only the Irish either —Cypriots, too.

PAT. Arabs and Jews.

MEG. Yes and what about them poor Indians and Africans? Have you heard of them? Same thing happened to them. But do you think Mr. de Valera could do something about this? I'm sure he could stop it if he wanted to.

OFFICER AND PAT [together]. Mr. de Valera. (*It's the first time they ever agreed about anything.*]

MEG. I always heard that Mr. de Valera was a wonderful man. They say he can speak seven languages.

PAT. It's a terrible pity that English or Irish are not among them, so as we'd know what he was saying in odd times.

PRINCESS GRACE [*who has been fiddling with his portable radio*]. Quiet everybody. Something's happened.

EVERYBODY [*asks*]. What?

PRINCESS GRACE [*continues*]. They've kidnapped an English soldier.

OFFICER. Turn the thing up so that we can hear it.

> PRINCESS GRACE *turns the radio up and gets a blast of music. Then he turns it back and we hear a low mumble of static—he interprets.*

PRINCESS GRACE. So he was kidnapped, it said. What was that? From a dance, I think. Yes—three men jumped from a motor car—they . . . dragged the soldier . . . made off in fast speed in the direction of the border.

OFFICER. Turn it off. Patrick, get them out of here.

PAT. I can't do that just at the moment without making a show of ourselves.

OFFICER. Then come outside with me.

> PAT *and the* OFFICER *go out.*

PRINCESS GRACE. Who's he?

MEG. He's the man come about the rent.

> PRINCESS GRACE *turns music up on the radio then goes.*

MR. MULLEADY. The poor boy—in his lonely cell—waiting all night for the screw coming for him in the morning.

TERESA. It would break your heart to be thinking about him.

MR. MULLEADY. I know just how he feels.

MEG. How do you know?

MR. MULLEADY. Well, I was inside myself.

MEG. Oh, I see.

MR. MULLEADY. My downfall was the *Pall Mall Gazette* in 1919.

MEG. The what?

MR. MULLEADY. The *Pall Mall Gazette*. It's a magazine. I saw an advertisement in it—it was for an Insurance Company. I put all my savings into this company and in return I was to receive an annuity of twenty pounds a year. Of course, when the annuity was due the value of money had declined. I had sold my youth all for that miserable twenty pounds a year. As a result I borrowed the Church funds but I was found out and sent to prison. I broke my poor mother's heart.

MEG. Well, I never caused my mother any sorrow—for I never knew her.

MR. MULLEADY. How very sad—you never had a mother.

MEG. I never heard of any living person that didn't have a mother—though there's plenty that has no fathers. I had one, but I never saw her.

MR. MULLEADY. Now I'm sentenced for life to this religious mechanic.

MEG. Anyway, are you going to sit all night there moaning about mothers? Did you brush your room?

MR. MULLEADY. I did not.

MEG. Well, go out and get a bottle of stout for me. It's all right, tell him to put it on the slate—you might as well make yourself useful—Teresa and I have a lot to do yet, getting this place tidy for all and sundry.

MR. MULLEADY *goes*.

TERESA. There's some awful strange people in this house, aren't there, Meg?

MEG. There's some awful strange people in the world.

TERESA. I like that gentle young man—there was no-one like him in the convent.

MEG. Do you mean Princess Grace?

TERESA. Yes, isn't it a funny name?

MEG. How long have you been out of the convent?

TERESA. I've just had the one job I told you about with that family in Drumcondra.

MEG. Why did you leave there? Did you half-inch something?

TERESA. What did you say?

MEG. Did you half-inch something?

TERESA. I never stole anything in my whole life.

MEG. There's no need to go mad about it—I never stole anything either. The grand chances I had—ah, I was young and foolish that time. God doesn't give us these chances twice in a lifetime.

TERESA. It wasn't that, Meg; there was a clerical student in the house.

MEG. Ah well, as far as that's concerned, you'll be a lot safer here. Do the nuns know you left that job?

TERESA. Oh no, they mightn't be too satisfied with me.

MEG. Well, don't say anything to Pat; it doesn't do to tell men everything. Here he comes.

    PAT *enters with* MONSEWER.

MEG. Oh, isn't it terrible, Pat; they are after refusing mercy to that poor boy in Belfast. He will be hanged tomorrow morning at eight o'clock.

TERESA. Wouldn't it break your heart to be thinking of him?

MONSEWER. It won't break my heart.

PAT [*aside*]. 'Course, it's not your neck they're breaking either.

MONSEWER. It does not make me unhappy. It does not make me unhappy, but proud. It makes me proud and happy to know that the old cause is not dead yet, and that there are still young men willing and ready to go out and die for Ireland.

PAT. I'd say that young man will be in the presence of the

Irish martyrs of eight hundred years ago a couple of minutes after eight tomorrow morning.

MONSEWER. He will. He will. With God's help, tomorrow morning he will be in the company of the heroes. It warms my heart to think of it.

MEG. Me life and yours.

MONSEWER. I would give all that I have in the wide world to stand in the place of that young man in Belfast Jail tomorrow morning. For Ireland's sake I would hang crucified in the town square.

PAT. Let's hope it would be a fine day for you.

MEG. Or you wouldn't get the crowd.

MONSEWER. I think he's very lucky.

PAT. It's a pity he didn't buy a sweepstake ticket. You were always a straight man, General, if I may call you by your Christian name. Well, all preparations are made for the guest.

MONSEWER. Good. Carry on. [*Exit.*]

> PAT *exits, singing* "*Had he died by Pearse's side or in the G.P.O.*"

TERESA. Wasn't that the ridiculous talk that old one had out of him about the boy being hung?

MEG. Well, Monsewer doesn't look at it like any ordinary person. Monsewer is very given to Ireland and to things of that sort.

TERESA. I think he's an old idiot.

MEG. An idiot? Monsewer was in all the biggest colleges of England, I'll have you know.

TERESA. It's all the same where he was. He is mad to say that the death of a young man made him happy.

MEG. Well, the boy himself said in court when they sentenced him to death that he was proud and happy to die for Ireland.

TERESA. He hasn't lived yet.

MEG. Have you?

TERESA. A girl of eighteen knows more than a boy of eighteen.

MEG [*sighs*]. They could easy do that. Poor lad. He gave no love to any, except to Ireland, and instead of breaking his heart for a girl, it was about the cause he was breaking it.

TERESA. Well, his white young neck will be broken to-morrow morning anyway.

MEG. Sure, we can't be thinking of it. It'd break our hearts. Let us have a bit of music. There's no need to mourn him before the time.

> *The hornpipe called "The Blackbird" is heard on the radio. They look at each other and* TERESA *smiles. She goes out on the floor and dances to the music. She offers her hand to* MEG, *inviting her to join the dance.* MEG *comes out, slowly and shyly at first, but in the finish the two are dancing opposite each other, lively and gay.*

THE RADIO . . . *The Blackbird* . . .

> *The door opens right unknownst to the two girls dancing, and a young man in British Army khaki battledress stands in the door.* TERESA *sees him first and it gives her a shock. She stops dancing.* MEG *follows* TERESA's *gaze to the door and she stops.*

SOLDIER Don't stop. I like dancing.

OFFICER. Keep your mouth shut and get up there.

> *He is quite at ease and smiling. He comes in with the* OFFICER *and another* MAN *behind him. They have their hands in the pockets of their raincoats.*

SOLDIER *sings:*

> There's no place on earth like the world.
> There's no place wherever you be,
> There's no place on earth like the world,
> That's straight up and take it from me.
>
> Never throw stones at your mother,
> You'll be sorry for it when she's dead,
> Never throw stones at your mother,
> Throw bricks at your father instead.
>
> The South and the North Poles they are parted,
> Perhaps it is all for the best,
> Till the H-bomb will bring them together—
> And there we will let matters rest.

ACT II

One door is guarded by the OFFICER, *the other by the*
VOLUNTEER. *The* SOLDIER *walks up and down whistling
to himself.*

SOLDIER [*plucking up courage*]. Hey! Hey!

> *There is no response. He whistles loudly. Both the*
> OFFICER *and the* VOLUNTEER *poke their heads round the
> door at the same time.*

SOLDIER. HALT!

> VOLUNTEER *halts.*

OFFICER. What's going on in here?

SOLDIER. Any chance of a cigarette?

OFFICER. Don't smoke.

> VOLUNTEER *shakes his head.*

SOLDIER. Oh.

> *They go. He walks again.*

VOLUNTEER. Hey!

SOLDIER. Yeah?

VOLUNTEER. You'll get a cup a tea in a minute.

SOLDIER. Smashing.

> *The* SOLDIER *whistles to himself. Suddenly a shrill blast
> brings in the two heads again.*

OFFICER. Well, what's the matter now?

SOLDIER. Nothing.

OFFICER. What's all the noise about?

SOLDIER. I just thought that she might be bringing my tea in.

OFFICER. Who's she?

SOLDIER. The one we saw at first, you know; bit of all right, eh?

No response. They go.

OFFICER [*to* VOLUNTEER]. Keep him covered. I'll go and see how the tea's coming along.

PRINCESS GRACE, RIO RITA, MULLEADY *and* WHORES
appear and try to see the prisoner.

PAT [*entering*]. Come on, out of here, you lot. You don't own the place.

PRINCESS GRACE. Why?

PAT. We're having the room fumigated. Out!

They go. PAT *calls* TERESA *in.*

Go on. Take it in to him now.

TERESA *goes into the room, with a tray.*

SOLDIER. Hallo. Cor, I was hoping I'd see you again.

TERESA. I was after bringing you a nice tea.

SOLDIER. Hey. I liked your dancing. The old foot-work.

TERESA. Thank you. [*She can't find a place for the tray.*]

SOLDIER. Going to have some with us?

TERESA. Don't stand there like an idiot. Don't you need it yourself? Your belly must be stuck to your back with hunger.

SOLDIER. Hey. Did you cook it for me yourself?

TERESA. Yes. You're lucky, Meg gave me two rashers.

SOLDIER. Good old Meg!

TERESA. She said you must have double the meal of a grown person because you have two jobs to do.

SOLDIER. What are they?

TERESA. To live and to improve, like all boys.

SOLDIER. Here. I'm older than you, I bet.

TERESA. I think you look like a boy.

SOLDIER. Look, I'm nearly nineteen.

TERESA. So am I.

SOLDIER. When were you born?

TERESA. January. Twenty-fifth of January. You?

SOLDIER. The eighteenth of August.

TERESA. So you see, I am older than you.

> PAT *walks up and down outside. She looks out and he winks at her. She sits down.*

TERESA. What name do we call you?

SOLDIER. Tell me yours first.

TERESA. Teresa.

SOLDIER. Teresa! That's real Irish, ain't it? I'm a Leslie.

TERESA. A Leslie?

SOLDIER. Got a fag?

TERESA. A what?

SOLDIER. A cigarette.

TERESA. No, thank you. I don't smoke.

SOLDIER. No, I mean . . . for me. You couldn't get me one, could you?

TERESA. Wait a minute, I think I have one on me. Look, it's only a bit crushed, Pat gave it to me though he knows I don't smoke. Here!

SOLDIER. I suppose you couldn't get me a packet.

TERESA. I'll get you twenty Afton.

SOLDIER. Oh no. I mean . . . thanks, anyway. Ten'll do.

TERESA. You don't fancy the Irish cigarettes?

SOLDIER. What? The old Aftons? Take hundreds of them with me when I goes home on leave.

TERESA. You shall have twenty of them. After all, you have the night before you.

He looks around at the bed.

Are you looking for something?

SOLDIER. No. Yes, an ashtray.

TERESA. Under the bed?

SOLDIER [*blushing*]. Well, I might have been looking for the in and the out, mightn't I?

TERESA. The in and the out?

SOLDIER. Well, I'm a prisoner, ain't I?

TERESA. I'd better go. Oh, the tray; they'll be needing it.

SOLDIER. Will you be back?

TERESA. I may be. I only work here, you know.

TERESA *goes.*

SOLDIER [*to* VOLUNTEER]. Excuse me, mister, but—

VOLUNTEER. Don't keep bobbing about.

SOLDIER. I'd like to have a—you know!

PAT. What's he saying?

VOLUNTEER. He wants a—to go round the back, sir.

PAT. Well, he can, can't he, surely?

VOLUNTEER. No, sir. I'm in the same plight myself, and I can't move from this door for another hour yet.

PAT. Why don't you both go?

VOLUNTEER. We'll have to ask the officer.

PAT. Well, I'll call him. Sir! Are you there, sir?

The OFFICER *appears.* PAT *whispers to him.*

[*To* AUDIENCE.] A man wants to go round the back and it's a military secret.

OFFICER. Right! Attention! Fall in! [*To* PAT.] You in front! Quick march! Halt! Right! You two guard the door! Silence!

TERESA *comes in quickly with the cigarettes.*

TERESA. Leslie!

OFFICER. What are you doing here?

TERESA. Where is he?

OFFICER. What is this man to you?

TERESA. Nothing, sir. I was just bringing him his cigarettes, sir.

OFFICER. Give them to me.

TERESA. But they're his, sir; he gave me the money for them.

PAT [*off*]. Attention! Quick march! At the double! One man relieved, sir.

The three come marching back into the room.

VOLUNTEER. What about me?

OFFICER. Silence!

TERESA. Where has he been?

PAT. Doing a job that neither you nor me nor anyone else could do for him.

TERESA. Leslie, I got you—

OFFICER. That's enough. Get along with you! About your business.

He takes PAT *aside.*

OFFICER. Is that girl all right?

PAT. Now, now, you shouldn't have your mind on that sort of thing and you on duty—

OFFICER. I mean will she keep her mouth shut?

PAT. Sure now, you know what women are about these things. Did you have a bit last night? But I don't think she'd fancy you somehow.

OFFICER. I'm asking if she's to be trusted.

PAT. You mean would she help your man to beat it?

OFFICER. Yes.

PAT. She'd do nothing to bring the police to the house, I'm sure of that. And as for helping him to get away, if I've got eyes in my head, she's all for keeping him here. It seems they're getting along very well.

OFFICER. Yes. A bit too well for my liking.

PAT. Well, sir, she's passing the time for him. Isn't it better to have him well entertained, than roaring and bawling and looking for a fight? Sure, they looked like two little budgeriguards to me.

OFFICER. This is no laughing matter, you idiot.

PAT [*to* AUDIENCE]. You know, there are two sorts of gunmen, the earnest, religious-minded ones, like you, and the laughing boys.

OFFICER. Like you.

PAT. Well, you know in the time of the troubles it was always the laughing boys who were the most handy with a skit.

OFFICER. Why?

PAT. Because it's not a natural thing for a man with a sense of humour to be playing with firearms and fighting. There must be something the matter with him.

OFFICER. There must be something the matter with you, then.

PAT. Of course there is. Give him the bloody cigarettes.

H.–D

The OFFICER *flaps them up and down in his hand, debating, when suddenly all the other characters rush on to the stage.*

MISS GILCHRIST. I heard them at the end of the street.

MEG. Have they gone past? Here they come.

PRINCESS GRACE. Look at 'em all. There's hundreds.

MEG. THOUSANDS!

PAT. What's going on? Yes, what's going on?

MEG. They're marching to the G.P.O. over the boy that's being hung tomorrow.

PAT. Oh sure, the procession.

TERESA. The poor boy, the poor boy.

They all come down to the footlights. The lights change so that you can only see their faces in spotlighting. The face of the SOLDIER *is picked out on the platform above. In the darkness the "Flowers of the Forest" is heard on the pipes.*

Sh! Here they come.

PAT [*as the pipes fade*]. There they go. It's like a funeral. Jim Larkin's funeral.

OFFICER. Plenty of police about.

MONSEWER. Plenty of banners. Another victim for occupied Ireland.

MEG. "England, the hangman of thousands. In Kenya, in Ireland, in Cyprus! In India! The World!"

MULLEADY. "Release the Belfast martyr!"

MEG. "We'll See Another Day When England Will Be That Low You Won't Be Able To Walk On Her!"

PRINCESS GRACE. "Eighteen Years of Age—in jail for Ireland!"—ah, the poor boy. Oh, the murdering bastards.

The faces watch the procession going.

SOLDIER. You know who they're talking about, don't you? 'Course all the papers twist it. That Irish fellow in Belfast Jail that's to be topped tomorrow morning. Did you read about him in the papers? We did. They was full of it where we were. Of course, most of our lads are National Servicemen, you know. I mean they're all about the same age as this young fellow that's going to be topped.

MEG. That's the end of it.

PAT. Ah well, thanks be to God it's not the way we all go.

MISS GILCHRIST. Is this the English boy? May I give him a little gift?

PAT. What is it?

MISS GILCHRIST. An article in a newspaper and as it's about his own Queen I thought he might like it.

OFFICER. What is it called?

MISS GILCHRIST. It is from the *Daily Express*. It is called "Within the Palace Walls". Here, I will read what it says on the cover. "Within the Palace Walls. So much is known of the Queen's life on the surface, so little about how her life is really run. But now this article has been written with the active help of the Queen's closest advisers."

SOLDIER. No thanks, ma'am, I don't go for that sort of mullarkey. Haven't you got something else?

MULLEADY. Evangelina!

MISS GILCHRIST. Who calls?

MULLEADY. Me! Me! Me! Me! Bookie! Please! Please!

MISS GILCHRIST. Well, if the boy doesn't want it.

MULLEADY. May I read on, please?

MISS GILCHRIST. Go on, Eustace.

MULLEADY. "Within the Palace Walls, because it is completely fresh, probing hitherto unreported aspects of her problems, this intriguing new serial lays before you the true pattern of the Queen's Life with understanding, intimacy, and detail." Oh! May I keep it, Miss Gilchrist?

PAT. Look at that, it's written by an Irishman—Dermot Morrah.

MEG. And she calls herself an Irishwoman, the silly old bitch.

MISS GILCHRIST. I have nothing against the Royal Family, I think they're lovely, especially Peter Townsend and Uffa Fox. I get every Sunday paper to follow them up. One paper contradicts another, so you put two and two together—and you might as well be sitting in the yacht with them. And there's that Mrs. Dale, she's a desperate woman, they even have an Irishman in it, a Mr. O'Malley, he keeps a hotel like you, Mr. Pat.

MULLEADY [singing].

> I'll get this paper every day.
> It will be my bible!

SOLDIER. Well, personally, mate, I'd sooner have the bleeding Bible. I read it once when I was on jankers.

MISS GILCHRIST. Is it true?

SOLDIER. It's blue, Mum.

MISS GILCHRIST. My favourite colour.

SOLDIER. You'd like it then, though the blue bits take a bit of sorting out from the dreary bits.

MISS GILCHRIST. May we sing to you?

MULLEADY and MISS GILCHRIST sing "Nobody Loves You Like Yourself".

MULLEADY AND MISS GILCHRIST [singing].

You read the Bible in its golden pages,
You read those words, and talking much of love,

You read the works of Plato and the sages,
They tell of Hope, and Joy and Peace and Love,
But I'm afraid it's all a lot of nonsense,
About as true as leprechaun or elf,
You realize, when you want somebody,
That there is no one loves you like yourself.

I did my best to be a decent person,
I drove a tram for Murphy, in 'thirteen,
I failed to pass my medical for the Army,
But loyally tried to serve my King and Queen.
Through all the trouble times I was no traitor,
Even when the British smashed poor mother's delph,
And when they left, I was a loyal Free-stater,
But I know there is no one loves you like yourself.

I really think us lower middle-classes
Get thrown around just like snuff at a wake,
Employers take us for a set of asses,
The rough they sneer at all attempts we make,
To have nice manners and to speak correctly,
And in the end we're flung upon the shelf,
We have no unions, cost of living bonus,
It's plain to see that no one loves you like yourself.

Bows and curtseys; they go off.

PAT [*at end of song*]. Come on, that's enough of that. Get along with you.

TERESA [*entering, whispering*]. Leslie!

SOLDIER. Did you get my cigarettes?

TERESA. I gave them to that officer. Did he never pass them on to you?

SOLDIER. No.

TERESA [*she swears in Irish*].

SOLDIER. Now, now, now, no swearing. Anyway, you should never trust the officers.

There is a blast on MONSEWER'S *pipes.*

SOLDIER. What the hell's that?

TERESA. It's Monsewer practising his pipes. He's going to play a lament tomorrow morning, for the boy in Belfast.

SOLDIER. He's got a lot of practising to do, hasn't he?

TERESA. Don't joke about it.

SOLDIER. I'm not joking. I feel sorry for the poor fellow, but that won't help him, will it?

TERESA. He's one of your noble gentlemen, anyway; he went to college with your king.

SOLDIER. With who?

TERESA. Your king.

SOLDIER. We ain't got one.

TERESA. Maybe he's dead now, but you had one once.

SOLDIER. No, we got a Duke now.

TERESA. Anyway, he left your lot and came over and fought for Ireland anyway.

SOLDIER. What did he want to do that for? Was somebody doing something to Ireland?

TERESA. Wasn't England, for hundreds of years?

SOLDIER. That was donkeys years ago. Anyway, every-body was doing something to someone in those days.

TERESA. And what about today? What about that young man in Belfast Jail?

SOLDIER. Well, you know, you can't let blokes go round shooting at coppers. I don't fancy coppers much myself, but you've got to have law and order. And a copper couldn't even walk his beat if everyone who didn't like him started taking pot-shots at him.

TERESA. In the six counties the police walk the beat in tanks and armoured cars.

SOLDIER. Look, if he was an Englishman he'd be hanged just the same.

TERESA. It's because of the English being in Ireland that he fought.

SOLDIER. And what about the Irish being in London? Thousands of them. Nobody's doing anything to them. . . . 'Course, that's London. That's where we should be, down the 'dilly on a Saturday night.

TERESA. You're as bad as the Dublin people here; they think they're great.

SOLDIER. Don't you come from Dublin, Teresa?

TERESA. No, I don't.

SOLDIER. Country yokel, are you, Teresa?

TERESA. I was reared in the convent at Ballymahon.

SOLDIER. I was reared in the Old Kent Road.

TERESA. Is that where your father and mother live?

SOLDIER. I ain't got none.

TERESA. You're not an orphan, are you?

SOLDIER. Yes, that's right. I'm one of the little orphans of the storm.

TERESA. I don't believe you.

SOLDIER. Well, actually my old lady ran off with a Pole, not that you'd blame her if you knew my old man.

MONSEWER *enters playing bagpipes.*

SOLDIER. The only good thing about those pipes is they don't smell.

MONSEWER. That wasn't too good, was it, Patrick?

PAT. No, sir, it wasn't.

MONSEWER. Never mind. We'll get there. I'll have it by tomorrow morning.

PAT. Yes, sir.

MONSEWER. I'd like to see the prisoner a moment.

PAT. Certainly, sir. [*He enters room.*] Now then. You come down here. To attention! Stand by your bed.

MONSEWER. What's she doing here? Fraternizing?

PAT. No, sir, not at the moment. She's just remaking the bed.

MONSEWER. Now, you, my boy, what's your name?

SOLDIER. Williams, sir. Leslie A.

MONSEWER. Stationed at?

SOLDIER. Armagh, sir.

MONSEWER. Did you like it?

SOLDIER. No, sir. What a dump! Everything shuts at ten. The place is dead. You can't get a drink on Sunday. I can't think why they ever sent us there.

MONSEWER. You see, Patrick, morale is bad.

PAT. Dreadful, sir.

SOLDIER. Excuse me, sir, can I ask you a question?

MONSEWER. Go ahead.

SOLDIER. What are those pipes for?

MONSEWER. These? To play, of course. They are the instrument of a noble and ancient race.

SOLDIER. I see. I never could get the hang of all this race lark business myself; much too complicated.

MONSEWER. This race lark, as you call it, is when a lot of people have lived in the same place for a very long time.

SOLDIER. Then I reckon our old Sergeant Major must be a race. He's been living at the old depot for nearly forty years.

MONSEWER. What regiment are you with?

SOLDIER. R.E.M.E., sir.

MONSEWER. Ah, you mean the Royal Electrical and Mechanical Engineers, a very good regiment, very good indeed.

SOLDIER [to PAT]. You know he's the spitting image of our old Colonel back at the depot. Same face, same voice. Gorblimey, I reckon it is him.

MONSEWER. Focail . . .

SOLDIER. He a Free Hungarian or something?

MONSEWER. Focailelle.

SOLDIER. What's that, garlic?

PAT *gestures to him to shut up.*

MONSEWER. Has he come here to make a mockery of a civilization that was old in the days of the Greeks?

SOLDIER. Did he say Greek? I know a Greek bloke who runs a café down the Edgware Road, smashing scoff, only thing is it gets a bit greasy, but mind you, the rosy lee and holy ghost is marvellous. Best anywhere in London.

MONSEWER. Rosy Lee. What abomination is this?

SOLDIER. C. of E., guv.

PAT. Cockney humour, sir.

MONSEWER. You can't even speak the Queen's English.

PAT. He can't even speak his own English.

SOLDIER. I can make myself understood everywhere. Don't matter whether I'm in Brixton or Hampstead or anywhere.

MONSEWER. No background, no tradition, nothing.

SOLDIER. Oh yes I have. They gave us all that at the Boys' Home. Cricket, team spirit, fair play—we took all that.

MONSEWER. Did you play cricket?

SOLDIER. Yes, sir. Do you like a game?

MONSEWER. Yes.

SOLDIER. Mind you, I couldn't get on with it at the Boys' Home. They gave us two sets of stumps, you see, and I'd always been used to one, chalked up on the old wall at home.

MONSEWER. That's not cricket, my boy.

SOLDIER. Now there you are, you see. Now you're what I call a cricket person and I'm what I call a soccer person. There's where your race lark comes in.

MONSEWER. Ah, cricket, by jove that takes me back. Fetch the pianist, Patrick. Strange how this uncouth youth has brought back half-forgotten memories of summers long past.

He sings "The Captains and the Kings".

> I remember in September
> When the final stumps were drawn,
> And the shouts of crowds now silent
> And the boys to tea have gone.
> Let us, oh Lord above us,
> Still remember simple things
> When all are dead who love us,
> Oh, the captains and the kings,
> When all are dead who love us,
> Oh, the captains and the kings.
>
> We have many goods for export
> Christian ethics and old port,
> But our greatest boast is that
> The Anglo-Saxon is a sport.
> When the darts game is finished
> And the boys their game of rings

And the draughts and chess relinquished,
Oh the captains and the kings,
And the draughts and chess relinquished,
Oh, the captains and the kings.

Far away in dear old Cyprus,
Or in Kenya's dusty land,
Where all bear the white man's burden,
In many a strange land,
As we look across our shoulder,
In West Belfast the school bell rings,
And we sigh for dear old England,
And the captains and the kings,
And we sigh for dear old England,
And the captains and thc kings.

In our dreams we see old Harrow,
And we hear the crow's loud caw,
At the flower show our big marrow
Takes the prize from Evelyn Waugh.
Cups of tea, or some dry sherry,
Vintage cars these simple things,
So let's drink up and be merry,
Oh, the captains and the kings,
So let's drink up and be merry,
Oh, the captains and the kings.

I stumbled in a nightmare,
All around Great Windsor Park,
And what do you think I found there
As I wandered in the dark.
'Twas an apple half-bitten,
And sweetest of all things,
Five baby teeth had written,
Of the captains and the kings,

Five baby teeth had written,
Of the captains and the kings.

By the moon that shines above us,
In the misty morn and night,
Let us cease to run ourselves down,
But praise God that we are white,
And better still are English,
Tea and toast and muffin rings,
Old ladies with stern faces,
And the captains and the kings,
Old ladies with stern faces,
And the captains and the kings.

Enter OFFICER. TERESA *hides under bed.*

PAT. Well, that's brought the show to a standstill.

OFFICER. Pat, get that old idiot out of here. Guard!

VOLUNTEER. Sir.

OFFICER. No one is to be allowed in here, do you understand? No ONE!

VOLUNTEER. Yes, sir. Sir, might I be relieved of my duties for just two minutes, sir, while I slip out the back . . .

OFFICER. No, certainly not. This place is like a rabbit warren with everyone skipping about.

MONSEWER. The laddie from headquarters. There you are!

OFFICER. Yes, here I am. I don't know quite how to put this, sir, but from now on I intend to have some discipline around here.

MONSEWER. Quite right, too.

OFFICER. I must ask you what you were doing in there?

MONSEWER. Inspecting the prisoner.

OFFICER. I'm afraid I must ask you to keep out of here.

MONSEWER. And I must ask you to remember my rank. I

know you're working under a strain at the moment, Captain, but—there's no need to treat me like an Empire Loyalist. You know where to find me when you need me, Patrick?

PAT. Very good sir.

MONSEWER. I'll be working on my plan. Chin up, sonny.

SOLDIER. Cheerio, sir.

OFFICER. Now, we've had enough of this nonsense. I'll check the room myself.

PAT. Yes, sir.

He sits on the bed and TERESA *yells.* PAT *coughs.*

SOLDIER. Can I ask you what you intend to do with me, guvnor?

OFFICER. Keep your mouth shut and no harm will come to you. Have you got everything you want?

SOLDIER. Oh yes, sir.

OFFICER. Right. Take over, Patrick. I'm going to the end of the street to check the other sentries.

PAT. Yes. Have you got the place well covered, sir?

OFFICER. Why?

PAT. It looks like rain.

OFFICER. No more tomfoolery, please.

Exit OFFICER. PAT *moves and stands outside the room.* TERESA *looks out from under the bed and calls* "Leslie."

SOLDIER. I'm not here. I've gone home.

TERESA. Have they gone?

SOLDIER. You wanted to stay with me, Teresa? Didn't you? Didn't you?

TERESA. No I didn't, I just didn't want him to see me. I'm going now.

SOLDIER. Don't go.

TERESA. Why?

SOLDIER. I—well, I like company.

TERESA. I shouldn't be here now; you heard what he said.

SOLDIER. Stay. I'll hide you if he comes back.

TERESA. Meg'll be wondering where I am.

SOLDIER. She told me she thought you was in the kitchen. Stay. Go on—stay and tell me a story—the Irish are great at that, aren't they?

TERESA. Well, not all of them—I'm not. I don't know any stories.

SOLDIER. Well, any story'll do. It doesn't have to be funny. It's just something to pass the time, ain't it?

TERESA. Yes. You've a long night ahead of you, and so has he.

SOLDIER. Who?

TERESA. You know, the boy in Belfast.

SOLDIER. He? Oh, don't start talking about that again, that'll spoil it.

TERESA. I'll tell you about when I was a girl in the convent.

SOLDIER. Yeah, that should be a bit of all right. Go on.

TERESA. Oh, it was the same as any other school, except you didn't go home—you played in a big yard which had a stone floor—you'd break your bones if you fell on it. But there was a big meadow outside the wall, and on Feast Days and holidays we were let out there. It was lovely. We were brought swimming a few times, too, but the nuns were awful careful, and if there was a man or a boy came within a mile of us we—well, we . . .

SOLDIER. Tell us, go on, go on, Teresa—after all we're grown-ups now, aren't we?

TERESA. We were not allowed to take off our clothes at all. You see, Leslie, even when we had our baths on Saturday nights they put shifts on the girls, even the little ones four or five years old.

SOLDIER. Did they?

TERESA. What did you have?

SOLDIER. Oh no, we never had anything like that. I mean, in our place we had all showers and we were sloshing water over each other and blokes shouting and screeching and making a row—it was smashing. Best night of the week, it was.

TERESA. Our best time was the procession we had for the Blessed Virgin on May Day—

SOLDIER. Procession for who?

TERESA. Shame on you, the Blessed Virgin. Anyone would think you were a Protestant.

SOLDIER. I am, girl.

TERESA. Oh, excuse me.

SOLDIER. That's all right. Never think about it myself.

TERESA. And anyway, on May Day we had this big feast.

SOLDIER. Was the scoff good?

TERESA. The . . . what?

SOLDIER. The grub! You don't understand what I'm talking about half the time, you know.

TERESA. Are you listening to me? Anyway, we had this procession, and I was with the mixed infants.

SOLDIER. What's a mixed infant?

TERESA. A little boy or girl under five years old. They were called mixed infants because until that time the boys and girls were mixed together.

SOLDIER. I wish I'd been a mixed infant.

TERESA. Do you want to hear my story? When the boys were six they were sent to the big boys' orphanage.

SOLDIER. You mean this place you were in was all orphans? Do you, Teresa? Were you one?

TERESA. I told you I was.

SOLDIER. No you didn't.

TERESA. Yes I did.

SOLDIER. Well, shake on it anyway.

They shake hands.

TERESA. I didn't believe your story.

SOLDIER. Well, it's true. Anyway, never mind. Tell us about this mixed infant job.

TERESA. He was on his own and he was crying like the rain. His father was dead, but his mother had run away. All the other boys and girls were laughing and shouting, but this one boy was on his own and nothing would stop him. So do you know what I did? I made a crown of daisies and a daisy chain to put round his neck and told him he was the King of the May. He forgot everything except that he was King of the May.

SOLDIER. Would you do that for me if I was a mixed infant?

TERESA. There's a clock striking somewhere in the city.

SOLDIER. I wonder what time it is?

TERESA. I don't know.

The bagpipes are heard.

SOLDIER. Will you give me a picture of yourself, Teresa?

TERESA. What for?

SOLDIER. I'd like to take it with me. I mean, they might take me away in the night and I might never see you again.

TERESA. Besides, I'm not Marilyn Monroe or Jayne Mansfield.

SOLDIER. Who wants a picture of them? They're all old.

TERESA. I haven't got a picture.

She pulls out a medal which she has round her neck.

SOLDIER. What's that?

TERESA. It's a medal.

SOLDIER. I'm doing all right, ain't I? In the army nine months and I get a medal.

TERESA. It's not that kind of medal.

She gives it him.

SOLDIER. It looks like you.

TERESA. Leslie! No, it's . . .

SOLDIER. Oh, it's that lady of yours.

TERESA. Yes, it's God's mother. She's the mother of everyone in the world, too. Will you wear it round your neck?

SOLDIER. If you'll put it on, Teresa.

She does. He tries to kiss her.

TERESA. Leslie! Don't.

SOLDIER. Now don't give me that old bull. Let's pretend we're on the films where all I have to say is "Let me", and all you have to say is—"Yes".

Music.

Come on, Teresa.

She is shy but he pulls her down towards the footlights and they sing and dance. The song is "I Will Give you a Golden Ball". On the last verse they walk towards the bed. Quick Blackout.

TERESA [*sings*].

I will give you a golden ball,
To hop with the children in the hall,
If you'll marry, marry, marry,
If you'll marry me.

SOLDIER [*sings*].

> I will give you the keys of my chest,
> And all the money that I possess,
> If you'll marry, marry, marry,
> If you'll marry me.

TERESA [*sings*].

> I will give you a watch and chain,
> To show the children in the lane,
> If you'll marry, marry, marry,
> If you'll marry me.

SOLDIER [*sings*].

> I will give you coins of gold,
> And as much and more as your hands can hold,
> If you'll marry, marry, marry,
> If you'll marry me.

TERESA [*sings*].

> I will bake you a big pork pie,
> And hide you till the cops go by,
> If you'll marry, marry, marry,
> If you'll marry me.

BOTH [*sing*].

> But first I think that we should see
> If we fit each other. Yes, I agree.

They lie on the bed. MISS GILCHRIST *runs on and into a spot.*

MISS GILCHRIST. They're away. My music, please.

She sings "Only a Box of Matches".

MISS GILCHRIST [*sings*].

> Only a box of matches
> I send, dear mother, to thee—
> Only a box of matches
> Across the Irish Sea.

I met with a Gaelic pawnbroker,
From Killarney's waterfalls,
In sobs he cried, "I wish I'd died;
The Saxons have stolen my balls."

MISS GILCHRIST *exits*. MEG *is heard calling*.

MEG. Teresa! Teresa!

VOLUNTEER. You can't go in there. Sir! [OFFICER *enters*.]

OFFICER. Yes.

VOLUNTEER. There's a woman trying to get in to him.

OFFICER. You can't go in there. Security forbids it.

VOLUNTEER. Common decency forbids it. He might not have his trousers on.

MEG. Auah, do you think I've never seen a man with his trousers off before?

OFFICER. I'd be surprised if you'd ever seen one with them on.

MEG. Thanks.

VOLUNTEER. He's a decent boy, for all he's a British soldier.

MEG. Ah, there's many a good heart beats under a khaki tunic.

VOLUNTEER. There's something in that. My own father was in the Royal Irish Rifles.

OFFICER. Mine was in the Inniskillings.

MEG. And mine was a parish priest.

OFFICER. God forgive you, woman. After saying that, I won't let you in at all.

MEG. Oh, I'm not that particular. I wasn't thinking of going in in the first place, but was going about my business till he stopped me.

PAT. Auah, let her go in, officer, just for a second. It'll cheer the poor boy up a bit.

OFFICER. I don't think we should. He's in our care and we're morally responsible for his spiritual welfare.

VOLUNTEER. Well, only in a temporal way, sir.

MEG. I only wanted to see him in a temporal way.

OFFICER [*to* VOLUNTEER]. Jesus, Mary and Joseph, but it would be a terrible thing for him to die with a sin of impurity on his—

SOLDIER [*running down into a spotlight*]. What's all this talk about dying? Die! Who's going to die?

MEG. We're all going to die, but not before Christmas we hope.

PAT. Now look what you've done. You'll have to let her in now. You should have been more discreet, surely.

OFFICER. Two minutes then.

> *The* OFFICER *and the* VOLUNTEER *move away. Lights up on the room.* TERESA *stands by the bed, frightened.*

MEG. She's there, she's been there all the time.

TERESA. I just came in to do the dusting, Meg.

> *She sits on the bed and turns from them.*

MEG. What's wrong with a bit of comfort on a dark night?

SOLDIER. Please, mum, what are they going to do with me?

MEG. You can take your hand off my knee.

SOLDIER. Sorry, mum.

MEG. I keep that for my business.

SOLDIER. Will you go out and ask those blokes why they pinched me? I don't think they know themselves.

MEG. Maybe they don't know, maybe a lot of people don't know . . . or maybe they've forgotten . . .

SOLDIER. I don't quite see what you mean.

MEG. You can't forget some things.

SOLDIER. Forget?

MEG. In Russell Street, in Dublin, right next to where I was born, the British turned a tank and fired shells into people's homes.

SOLDIER. I suppose it was war, missus.

MEG. Yes, it was war. Do you know who it was against?

SOLDIER. No, missus.

MEG. Old men and women, the bedridden and the cripples, the mothers with their infants.

SOLDIER. Why them?

MEG. Everybody that was able to move had run away.

SOLDIER. That was hard luck, missus.

MEG. In one room they found an old woman, her son's helmet and gas mask were still hanging on the wall. He had died fighting on the Somme.

SOLDIER. I don't know nothing about it, lady.

MEG. Would you like to hear more? Then listen.

She sings the song "Who Fears to Speak of Easter Week".

MEG [*sings*].

Who fears to speak of Easter Week,
That week of famed renown,
When the boys in green went out to fight,
The forces of the Crown.

With Mausers bold, and hearts of gold,
The Red Countess dressed in green,
And high above the G.P.O.
The rebel flag was seen.

Then came ten thousand khaki coats,
Our rebel boys to kill,

Before they reached O'Connell Street,
Of fight they got their fill.

They had machine guns and artillery,
And cannon in galore,
But it wasn't our fault that e'er one
Got back to England's shore.

For six long days we held them off,
At odds of ten to one,
And through our lines they could not pass,
For all their heavy guns.

And deadly poisoned gas they used,
To try and crush Sinn Fein,
And burnt our Irish capital,
Like the Germans did Louvain.

They shot our leaders in a jail,
Without a trial they say,
They murdered women and children,
Who in their cellars lay.

And dug their grave with gun and spade,
To hide them from our view,
Because they could neither kill nor catch,
The rebel so bold and true.

The author should have sung that one.

PAT. That is if the bleeding thing has an author.

SOLDIER. He doesn't mind coming over here and taking
our money.

OFFICER. Be Jesus, wait till he comes home. We'll give him
making fun of the movement.

SOLDIER. He's too bleeding anti-British.

OFFICER. Too anti-Irish you mean.

MEG. Ah, he'd sell his country for a pint.

PAT. And put up his hands and thank the Almighty God that he had a country to sell.

SOLDIER. Author, author.

MONSEWER. Author!

PAT. He might as well show up; it's his only bleeding chance of getting a curtain call. A lot he cares.

   Rock and Roll. Everybody dances. MUSICIAN *enters.*

MUSICIAN. Hey, Leslie!

SOLDIER. What?

MUSICIAN. Have you seen this?

SOLDIER. Throw it down.

   He throws a newspaper on to the stage.

TERESA. What is it?

SOLDIER. The evening paper, isn't it? [*He reads.*] "The Government of Northern Ireland have issued a statement that they cannot find a reason for granting a reprieve in the case of the condemned youth." Here! I've got my name in the papers. 'Private Leslie Alan Williams', that's me! Look at that!

PAT. You want to read a bit further.

MULLEADY. Yes, read on—

MISS GILCHRIST. I'm afraid it's possible—it's likely—that you'll be shot.

SOLDIER. Who are you?

MISS GILCHRIST. I am a sociable worker. Have you your testament?

SOLDIER. I hope so.

MISS GILCHRIST. He is an exile, poor lad. I feel for him, like a mother.

   Begins to sing, "Only a Box of Matches, I send, Dear Mother, to Thee".

SOLDIER. Shut up, this is serious. [*Reads.*] "In a statement today delivered to all newspaper offices and press agencies . . . he has been taken as a hostage . . ." that's me, a hostage! "If . . . executed . . . the Irish Republican Army declare that Private Leslie Alan Willams will be shot . . . will be shot . . . as a reprisal". [*Turns to the others.*] Does it really mean they're going to shoot me?

MULLEADY. I'm afraid so.

SOLDIER. Why?

MONSEWER. You're the hostage.

SOLDIER. I've done nothing wrong.

OFFICER. It's war.

SOLDIER. Would none of you let me free?

They all look at him.

Well, you crowd of bleeding— Give me some music, please.

He sings "I am a Happy English Lad".

I am a happy English lad
I love my royalty
And if they were short a penny on a packet of fags,
Now they'd only have to ask me.

I love old England in the east
I love her in the west
From Jordan's streams to Derry's Walls,
I love old England best.

I love my dear old Notting Hill
Wherever I may roam,
But I wish those bleeding Nigger-boys
Were kicked out and put back home.

CURTAIN

ACT III

PAT PAT, MISS GILCHRIST *and* MEG *are sitting drinking. The* VOLUNTEER *and the* OFFICER *are standing ground over* LESLIE.

PAT [*sings,* MISS GILCHRIST *joining in with him.*]

> On the fifteenth day of November,
> Just outside the town of Macroom,
> The 'Tans in their big Crossley tenders,
> Came roaring along to their doom.

MEG. Shut up, the two of you, or you'll have that Holy Joe down on us.

PAT. Who are you talking about?

MEG. That I.R.A. general, or whatever he is.

PAT. Him a general—in the old days we wouldn't have had him as a batman. He's no more than a messenger anyway. Have some whisky, Miss Gilchrist?

MISS GILCHRIST. Oh no, thank you, Mr. Pat.

MEG. She doesn't want it.

PAT. Get it down!

MEG. I heard they're all generals nowadays.

PAT. Like their mothers before them. You are speaking to a man who was a captain at the time of the troubles, Miss Gilchrist.

MEG. Fine bloody captain he was.

MISS GILCHRIST. Really.

PAT. Captain of "E" Company, second battalion, Dublin Brigade. Monsewer was the commandant.

MEG. "E" Company, who are they?

PAT. You've heard of A B C D E, I suppose?

MEG. Certainly I have.

PAT. Well!

MISS GILCHRIST. Wasn't that nice! It must be a lovely thing to be a captain.

PAT. Will you let me get on with my story?

MEG. I defy anyone to stop you.

PAT. Leslie, it was in Russell Street in Dublin.

MEG. I've already told him.

PAT. Give us a bloody drink.

MEG. Get it yourself.

MISS GILCHRIST. Please go on.

PAT. Oh well, give us a drink. [*They drink.*] It was at Mullingar, on the field of battle, that I lost my leg.

MEG. You told me it was at Cork.

PAT. No matter what I told you, it was at Mullingar, in the Civil War.

MISS GILCHRIST. Well, if that's the kind of war you call a Civil War, I wouldn't like to see an uncivil one!

PAT. What a battle! The fight went on for three days without cease.

MISS GILCHRIST. And what happened to your poor left foot, Mr. Pat?

PAT. It wasn't me left foot, but me right foot. Don't you know your left foot from your right? Don't you know how to make the sign of the cross?

MISS GILCHRIST. I do, thank you, but I don't make it with my feet.

PAT. What does it matter, left or right? There were good men lost on both sides. Ah, it was a savage and barbarous battle, and they had Lewis guns, Thompsons, land mines. All we had were rifles and revolvers. The town was nothing but red fire and black smoke and the dead piled high on the roads.

MEG. You told me there was only one man killed.

PAT. I told you that?

MEG. And he was the County Surveyor out measuring the road and not interfering with politics one way or another.

PAT. You're a liar.

MEG. You told me that both sides claimed him for their own when the fighting was over—I've seen the Celtic crosses on either side of the road, where they put up memorials to him.

PAT. It's all the same what I told you.

MEG. That's your story when you're drunk, anyway. Of course, like every other man, that's the only time you tell the truth.

PAT. Have you finished?

MEG. No! Begod, if whisky and beer were at pre-war prices the Father of Lies would be out of a job.

PAT. I lost me leg anyway, didn't I? Did I or did I not?

MEG. You lost the use of it, I know that.

MISS GILCHRIST. These little lovers' quarrels!

MEG. You keep out of it, you silly old get.

PAT. I lost me leg anyway, and these white-faced loons with their trench coats, berets and teetotal badges have no right to call themselves members of the I.R.A.

MISS GILCHRIST. They're only lads.

MEG. He begrudges them their bit of sport now he's old and beat himself.

PAT. What sport is there in that dreary loon we have round here?

MEG. They've as much right to their drilling and marching, their revolvers and generals and sacrifices and white horses and wounds and last dying words and glory as you had.

PAT. I'm not saying they haven't, did I?

VOLUNTEER. Oh, yes, you did, Pat.

MISS GILCHRIST. I heard you distinctly.

MEG. Weren't you young yourself once?

PAT. That's the way they talk to you.

MISS GILCHRIST. I always say that a general and a bit of shooting makes you forget your troubles.

MEG. Sure, it takes your mind off the cost of living.

MISS GILCHRIST. A poor heart it is that never rejoices.

PAT. You keep out of this, Leslie. Watch him, Feargus. Anyway, they've no right to be going up to the border and kidnapping—

They all look round at LESLIE.

MEG. They have as much right to leave their legs and feet up in the border as you had to leave yours at Mullingar or Cork or wherever it was. Sit down, you shadow of a whore's ghost, and let's have a drink in peace. [*They drink.*]

MISS GILCHRIST *takes a drink to* LESLIE.

VOLUNTEER. You've been warned before.

PAT [*to* MISS GILCHRIST]. Move away. You're coming on to be making smart remarks like that to a poor cripple man that never harmed anyone in his life.

MEG. Away with you.

PAT. Let alone the years I did in Mountjoy, incarcerated with the other Irish patriots, God help me.

MEG. Ah, Mountjoy and the Curragh Camp were universities for the like of you. But I'll tell you one thing and that's not two, the day you gave up work to run this house for Monsewer, and entertain the likes of her, you became a butler—a Republican butler, a half-red footman —a Sinn Fein skivvy—

MISS GILCHRIST. What a rough-tongued person.

PAT. Go on, abuse me—your own husband that took you off the streets on a Sunday morning, when there wasn't a pub open in the city.

MEG. Go and get a mass said for yourself. The only love you had you kept for Mother Ireland and leaving honest employment.

PAT. Why do you stop with me so?

MEG. God knows.

SOLDIER *sings to himself*. MISS GILCHRIST *joins in*.

MISS GILCHRIST. Do you hear the poor lamb, keening to himself? The exiled boy! Ochone! Ochone! And it's a coffin of white planks they'll be bringing him before long. Ochone! Ochone!

MEG. What language is that she's talking?

PAT. Italian. Be quiet, you queer old bird—have a drink!

MISS GILCHRIST. Oh, Mister Pat, God increase you.

SOLDIER [*sings*]. Rule Britannia, Britannia rules the waves.

PAT. Move over there if you're going to keep on moaning.
   [*To* SOLDIER] Hey!

MEG. I don't want her here.

SOLDIER. Yes!

PAT. If you must sing, sing something modern. Not Rule Britannia.

SOLDIER *is silent.*

You know, something cheerful and up to date.

SOLDIER. I can't think of anything.

VOLUNTEER. Then shut up.

MISS GILCHRIST. I know what it is to be an exile. Dublin is not my home.

MEG. That's one thing in its favour.

MISS GILCHRIST. I came here to run a house, Mr. Pat.

MEG. I told you what she was.

MISS GILCHRIST. It was in a very respectable district, you know, and we only took in clerical students. They were lovely boys, much more satisfactory than the medical students.

PAT. Ah yes, the medicals is more for the beer.

MISS GILCHRIST. Of course, my boys had renounced the demon drink. Being students of Divinity, they had better things to do.

MEG. What things?

PAT. Now, Meg! You know what they go in for, reading all about— "This one lay with that one", and "Mat begat Pat", and that old fellow lying with his daughters—

MEG. And getting the best of eating and drinking, too. It's a wonder they're anyway controllable at all.

MISS GILCHRIST. Sometimes they were not. Ah, life has its bitter memories.

PAT. Have a drink.

MISS GILCHRIST [*crying*]. Thank you. Since then I have had recourse to good works. Recalling the sinner, salvaging his soul.

MEG. We'll leave his soul out of it, whatever about your own, or I'll set fire to you.

MISS GILCHRIST. Our Blessed Lord said, "Every cripple has his own way of walking, so long as they don't cause strikes, rob, steal, or run down General Franco." Those are my principles.

MEG. Your principle is nothing but a pimp.

MISS GILCHRIST. To whom are you referring?

MEG. That creeping Jesus in the fifth floor back.

MISS GILCHRIST. Oh, you mean Mr. Mulleady?

MEG. I do.

MISS GILCHRIST. But he is a fonctionnaire.

MEG. Is that what they call it nowadays?

MISS GILCHRIST. I strove to save him, together we wrestled —against the Devil; but now I am more interested in this soldier's soul. [Sings.] I love my fellow creatures.

MEG. Leave that soldier's soul alone.

PAT. Leave him alone, he's too young for you.

MISS GILCHRIST. I'm as pure as the driven snow.

MEG. You weren't driven far enough.

PAT. Hey, Feargus.

VOLUNTEER. Captain.

PAT. Have a drink.

VOLUNTEER. Thanks!

PAT. Give him one as well.

SOLDIER. Here, it's all very well you coming the old acid and giving me all this old buck about nothing happening to me, but I'm not a complete bloody fool, you know.

PAT. Drink your beer.

SOLDIER. What have I ever done to you that you should shoot me?

PAT. What have you ever done for us? I'll tell you a little story. In the time of the famine, when our people were dying here like flies and your old Queen, Victoria was her name, she sends a five pound note to the famine fund, and just so they won't misunderstand her and take her for a rebel or something, she sends by the same post five pounds to the Battersea Dog's Home. Now you just think about that.

MEG. Good God, Pat, that was when Moses was in the Fire Brigade.

PAT. Let him think about that.

MISS GILCHRIST. They might have given us this island that we live on for ourselves.

SOLDIER. Can I ask you one thing, man to man? Why didn't they tell me why they took me?

PAT. Didn't they?

SOLDIER. No.

PAT. Well, there's a war going on in the North of Ireland. You were a soldier. You were captured.

SOLDIER. All right, so I'm captured. So I'm a prisoner of war.

PAT. Yes.

SOLDIER. Well, you can't shoot a prisoner of war!

PAT. Agreed! Who said anything about shooting?

SOLDIER. What about that announcement in the papers?

PAT. Bluff. Haven't you everything you could wish for? A bottle of stout, a new girl friend bringing you every class of comfort.

SOLDIER. Yes, till that bloke in Belfast is topped in the morning, then it'll be curtains for poor old Williams and I'm due for a week-end's leave an' all.

PAT. It's all bluff, propaganda! All they'll do is hold you for a few days.

MEG. And they might give him a last-minute reprieve.

SOLDIER. Who, me?

MEG. The boy in Belfast Jail, poor lad.

SOLDIER. Some hopes of that.

PAT. The British Government may be thinking twice about it now that they know we've got you.

VOLUNTEER. They know that if the Belfast martyr dies, their own man here will be plugged.

SOLDIER. And plug you!

PAT [*to* VOLUNTEER]. Be quiet, idiot, look how you've upset him! Take no notice of his nonsense.

SOLDIER. You're as barmy as him if you think that what's happening to Private Leslie Williams is upsetting the British Government. I suppose you think they're all sitting round in their West End clubs with handkerchiefs to their eyes, dropping tears into their double-whiskies. Yeah, I can just see it, the old Secretary of State for War waking his missus up in the night, "Oh, Isabel Cynthia," he'll say, "I can't get a wink of sleep wondering what's happening to that poor bleeder, Williams."

MISS GILCHRIST *cries*.

MISS GILCHRIST. Poor boy! Do you know, I think they ought to put his story in the *News of the World*. Ah, we'll be seeing you on the telly yet. Yes, he'll be famous like that Diana Dorn—or the other one who cut up his victim and threw the bits out of an aeroplane. Now, he has a serial running somewhere.

SOLDIER. I always heard the Irish were barmy. But that's going it, that is.

PAT. Eh, let's have a drink. [*Calls*.] Feargus!

H.—F

VOLUNTEER. Sir! I can't leave my post.

SOLDIER. Here, mum, listen—

PAT [*to* LESLIE]. Now, you stay where you are. I'm going to fix you. Here, hold this. [*Gives him a bottle.*] Now, I'm going to draw a circle round you, see, like that. Now you move outside that and you're a dead man. Have you got that?

MISS GILCHRIST [*sings*].

> Just say there is no other
> To take the place of mother,
> And kiss her dear sweet lips for me—

SOLDIER [*moving out of circle*]. Hey.

PAT. Yes! Now, I told you.

SOLDIER. I bet that fellow in Belfast wouldn't want me to be plugged.

PAT. Certainly he wouldn't.

SOLDIER [*moving out*]. What good's it going to do him?

PAT. Inside! That's right! Sure and it won't do him any good.

MEG. When the boy's dead, what good would it be to croak this one? It wouldn't bring the other back to life now, would it?

SOLDIER. What a caper! I'm just walking out of a dance hall—

PAT. Walk in.

SOLDIER [*back inside*]. Then this geezer nabs me. "What do you want?" I says. "Information," he says. "I ain't got no information," I says, "apart from me name and number and the addresses of the girls who work in the N.A.A.F.I." "Right," says this bloke, "we're taking you to Dublin; our Intelligence men want to see you."

PAT. "Intelligence!" Holy Jesus, wait till you meet 'em. This fellow here's an Einstein compared to 'em.

SOLDIER. Well, when will I be meeting 'em?

PAT. They'll be coming tomorrow morning to ask you a few questions.

SOLDIER. Yes, my last wishes, I suppose!

PAT. I've told you before not to be such an idiot.

VOLUNTEER. He's told you.

MISS GILCHRIST [sings].

> I have no mother to break her heart
> I have no father to take my part.

PAT. Ah, don't be tormenting the life out of me with your moaning, woman. Sit up there in that circle. Leslie, come and sit here. That old idiot would put years on you.

MISS GILCHRIST [as she goes]. I'll have you know I had my voice trained by an electrocutionist.

MEG. It sounds like it.

VOLUNTEER. It's neither this nor that, commandant, but if you're taking charge of the prisoner, I'll carry out me other duties and check the premises.

PAT. Do that.

VOLUNTEER. It's only a thick would neglect his duty, sir.

PAT. Ah sure, now, you may be blamed, Einstein, but you never will be shamed.

VOLUNTEER. I hope not, sir. Of course, God gives us the brains; it's no credit to ourselves.

PAT. Well, without coming the sergeant-major on you, will you get on with what you came for?

VOLUNTEER. I will sir, directly.

He salutes smartly and marches off.

H.–F*

PAT. Sit down.

SOLDIER *sits by* PAT.

MISS GILCHRIST. I have such a thirst on me, I think it must be the singing. You haven't—[*she looks under the table*] oh, Mr. Pat, you gave that twelve of stout a very quick death.

PAT. You could sing that if you had an air to it. Leslie, pop down to the corner and get us a dozen of stout.

SOLDIER. Right you are, sir.

PAT. The corner shop, mind.

SOLDIER. Yes, guv.

VOLUNTEER [*entering*]. Get back there! Into the circle! Where the hell do you think you're going?

SOLDIER. He told me to—

MEG. Now, Pat, you're only going to get the boy into trouble.

PAT. Right! Attention, quick march! Stand in your circle. Right!

The VOLUNTEER *marches over to* PAT.

No, you go and sit in the circle. Leslie, you come and sit over here.

SOLDIER. You just told me to—

PAT. Never mind what I told you. Come and sit here a minute.

SOLDIER [*in circle*]. You're just leading me up the garden path, sending me out for beer, you are. An' all of a sudden I'll look round and cop a bullet in my head. Anyway, I'll tell you this much, an Englishman can die as well as an Irishman or anybody else in the world.

PAT. Don't give me all that ould stuff about dying. There's no danger of your dying this next fifty years—barring you get a belt of an atom bomb, God bless you. Come and sit down.

SOLDIER *comes.*

Finish your drink.

SOLDIER. Do you know, Paddy, up till now I've proper enjoyed myself.

PAT. 'Course you have. Good luck to you, so, cheers!

SOLDIER. You know how it is.

SOLDIER *begins to sing "When Irish Eyes are Smiling". The others join in.*

[*Aside.*] Yeah, I've had a real good time, I have, better than the square bashing.

PAT. Sure thing!

MISS GILCHRIST [*sings*].

I have no mother to break her heart
I have no father to take my part.

MEG. She's off again.

MISS GILCHRIST AND SOLDIER [*sing*].

I have one friend and a girl is she.
And she'd lay down her life for McCaffery.

MISS GILCHRIST. Jesus, Mary and Joseph, I feel for this boy as if I were his mother.

MEG. That's remarkable, that is.

MISS GILCHRIST. It would be more remarkable if I were his father.

MEG. Were his father? How many of you is there? I never heard you were married.

MISS GILCHRIST. You never heard the Blessed Virgin was married.

MEG. That was done under the Special Powers Act by the Holy Ghost.

MISS GILCHRIST. I repulse your prognostications. It would answer you better [*she points to the floor*] to go and clean your carpet.

MEG. How dare you! Men of good taste have complicated me on that carpet. Away, you scruff-hound, and thump your craw with the other hypocrites.

MISS GILCHRIST. Pray, do not insult my religiosity.

MEG. Away, you brass.

MISS GILCHRIST. I stand fast by my Lord, and will sing my hymn now.

[*Sings.*]

> I love my dear Redeemer,
> My creator, too, as well.
> And oh, that filthy Devil,
> Should stay below in Hell.
> I cry to Mr. Dulles,
> Please grant me this great boon,
> Don't muck about, don't muck about,
> Don't muck about with the moon.
>
> I am a little Christ-ian,
> My feet are white as snow.
> And every day my prayers I say,
> For Empire lamb I go.

PAT. No wonder, with the price of beef.

MISS GILCHRIST.

> I cry unto Macmillan,
> That multi-racial coon,

I love him and those above him,
But don't muck about with the moon.
Don't muck about, don't muck about,
Don't muck about with the moon.

MEG. Get off the stage, you castle Catholic bitch.

MISS GILCHRIST. She is a no-class person. Things haven't been the same since the British went.

SOLDIER. That's a very kindly song you just sang, mum. Can you tell me what those kindly bastards are going to do me in for?

MEG. Maybe you voted wrong.

SOLDIER. I'm too young to have a vote for another three years.

MEG. Well, what are you poking your nose in our affairs for?

SOLDIER. In what affairs? I never knew anything about Ireland or Cyprus, or Kenya or Jordan or any of those places.

OFFICER [*entering*]. You may learn very shortly with a bullet in the back of your head.

Enter PRINCESS GRACE, RIO RITA, MULLEADY *and the* WHORES.

PRINCESS GRACE AND WHORES. Oh, no! It's not his fault.

MULLEADY. Whose fault is it then?

MISS GILCHRIST. It's the Government's fault.

PRINCESS GRACE. Poor boy!

MULLEADY. He should never have been brought here. It means trouble. I've been feeling it all day! It's illegal.

MISS GILCHRIST. Eustace? What are you doing with those persons?

MULLEADY. Are we speaking now, Miss Gilchrist? That's a

change. Ever since you've been interested in this young man's soul, a Civil Servant's soul means nothing to you.

MISS GILCHRIST. What has happened to you?

MULLEADY. You might as well be out of the world as out of the fashion.

PRINCESS GRACE. We've made a pact.

MEG. What are they up to?

PAT. I wouldn't trust them as far as I could fling them.

MULLEADY. Yes, you can't do what you like with us.

PRINCESS GRACE. You'll find out. For those who don't understand, we'll sing our ancient song. Uncle!

RIO RITA, MULLEADY and PRINCESS GRACE sing "When Socrates in Ancient Greece".

When Socrates in Ancient Greece
Sat in his Turkish bath,
He scrubbed himself, and rubbed himself,
And steamed both fore and aft.

He sang the song the sirens sang,
With Swinburne and Shakespeare,
We're here because we're queer
Because we're queer because we're here.

The highest people of the land
Are for or they're against,
It's all the same thing at the end,
A piece of sentiment.

From Swedes so tall to Arabs small
They answer with a leer,
We're here because we're queer
Because we're queer because we're here.

PRINCESS GRACE. The trouble we had getting that past the nice Earl of Scarbrough.

MISS GILCHRIST [*at end of song*]. Leslie, come away. This is not fit company for an innocent boy.

SOLDIER. No, mum.

MISS GILCHRIST. Leave off this boy. I'm sure there's a lot of good in him and he is not used to prostitutes, male, female or Wiston Mail.

MEG. Get out, you dirty low things. A decent whore can't get a shilling with 'em.

PRINCESS GRACE. Oh, Meg Dillon, you're very bigoted.

MEG. Don't use language like that here.

PRINCESS GRACE. Ta, ta, Leslie.

MISS GILCHRIST. Leave him. This boy is not a ponce.

SOLDIER. No, I'm a builder's labourer; at least I was.

MISS GILCHRIST. Honest toil.

SOLDIER. It's a mug's game.

MISS GILCHRIST. Oh my boy! Music, please.

They sing duet to the tune of Rolling Home to Merry England, SOLDIER *speaking his lines.*

	Would you live on woman's earnings?
	Would you give up work for good?
	For a life of prostitution,
SOLDIER.	Yes, too bloody true, I would.
MISS GILCHRIST.	Would you have a kip in Soho?
	Would you be a West End ponce?
SOLDIER.	I'm fed up with pick and shovel,
	And I'd like to try it once.
MISS GILCHRIST.	Did you read the Wolfenden
	Report on people like these?

SOLDIER.   Yes, gorblimey it was moving—
[*To* MULLEADY.] Can I borrow your copy, please?

                  Well, at this ponce business
                  I think I'll have a try.
                  And I'll drop the English coppers,
                  They are the best money can buy.

MISS GILCHRIST.   Goodbye, my son, God bless you,
                  Say your prayers each morn and night,
                  And send home your poor old mother,
                  A few quid—her widow's mite.

Enter TERESA.

TERESA [*softly on stairs*]. Leslie!

VOLUNTEER. You can call me Feargus.

PAT [*to* VOLUNTEER]. Come out of that.

TERESA. Leslie!

PAT [*to* VOLUNTEER]. Psst. Psst. Come out of that or you'll have us in trouble.

VOLUNTEER. What?

PAT. Attention! On guard! Now take off the lights and give them a chance.

MEG, PAT, MISS GILCHRIST, VOLUNTEER, *exeunt.*

TERESA. Leslie!

SOLDIER. I'm here.

TERESA. That strict officer is coming back to relieve Pat and I won't get a chance of a word with you.

SOLDIER. Well, what do you want?

TERESA. Don't be so narky. I just wanted to see you.

SOLDIER. Well, you'd better take a good look, hadn't you?

TERESA. What's eating you? I only wanted to talk to you, that's all.

SOLDIER. You haven't got much time, have you? Because I mightn't be able to talk so well with a hole right through me head.

TERESA. Musha! Don't be talking like that.

SOLDIER. Why not? Eh, why not?

TERESA. I came to see if you wanted a cup of tea.

SOLDIER. No, thanks, I've just had a barrel of beer.

TERESA. I'll go.

SOLDIER. Just before you go, don't think you've taken me for a complete bloody fool, will you? All this tea and beer lark. You even obliged me with that [*indicates bed*] meal!

TERESA. For God's sake.

SOLDIER. Well, go and look out of that window. Can you see that man on the corner? Another one at the door opposite? There are more than these two idiots doing guard on me. Look at those two by that archway, pretending they're lovers. That should be right up your street, pretending they're lovers! That's a laugh!

TERESA. It's not my fault. I wasn't pretending.

SOLDIER. How can I believe you and your blarney?

TERESA. The boys won't harm you. Pat told me himself they only wanted to question you, and to frighten the British about the boy in Belfast.

SOLDIER. Do you think he's going to tell you the truth, or even me? After all, if you really . . . if you really felt sorry for me you might shout to the police, mightn't you?

TERESA. I'm not an informer.

SOLDIER. Don't I know it. How long have I got? What time is it?

TERESA. It's not eleven yet. I heard the quarter bell go in the city.

SOLDIER. They'll just be waking up at home, fellows will be coming out of the dance halls.

TERESA. Look at that old fellow half-jarred, sobering up for fear of what herself will say when he gets in at the door.

SOLDIER. Back home, couple of hundred miles away, might be on another bloody planet.

TERESA. Look at that, the chip shop is still open. I could pretend to go for some chips. I could . . .

SOLDIER. I don't want any chips. Could you eat if you knew you were for it? You're thinking of that poor bastard in Belfast. What about me?

TERESA. God help us all.

SOLDIER. What about me—here, now?

TERESA. If I really thought they'd do anything to you, I'd . . .

SOLDIER. If you thought. I'm a hostage, you know what that means? What's the point of taking a hostage if you don't mean to do him in?

TERESA. Leslie, if they do come for you, shout to me.

SOLDIER. Shout! I wouldn't get the chance. If they come . . .

TERESA. Well, I can't be sure. Pat said . . .

SOLDIER. Oh go away and leave me in peace. At least that bloke in Belfast has peace, and tomorrow he'll have nuns and priests and the whole works to see him on his way.

TERESA. I'll do anything for you, Leslie. What do you want?

SOLDIER. I don't want anything. I'll do the best I can on my own. Maybe I'll meet that Belfast geezer on the other side. We can have a good laugh together then.

TERESA. Here's that officer coming now. I've got to go.

SOLDIER. Teresa!

TERESA. Yes.

SOLDIER. I know I wasn't much good to you—but say "goodbye" properly, eh?

TERESA *goes to his arms.*

If I should get away, come and see me in Armagh.

TERESA. I will, Leslie.

SOLDIER. I'd like all the blokes in the billet to see you. 'Cos they've all got pictures on the walls—well, I never had any pictures, but now I've got you. Then we'd go to Belfast and have a bloody good time together.

TERESA. It would be lovely, astore.

SOLDIER. I'm due for a week-end's leave.

TERESA. I could pay my own way too.

SOLDIER. No, you need not.

TERESA. But I will . . . They're coming.

She goes. PAT *and* OFFICER *are on the stairs.*

OFFICER. What's she doing? Sleeping with him?

PAT. Mind your own business, she's not interfering with you. You should be in bed now, girl. Where are you going?

TERESA. I was going to the chip shop, for some chips for him.

OFFICER. You can't go out there now.

PAT *quietens him.*

PAT. It's too late, girl.

TERESA. It's only eleven.

PAT. It's nearer one.

TERESA. It's not the truth you're telling me.

PAT. Didn't you hear the bell strike?

TERESA. I did.

OFFICER. Enough talk. Get her to her room or I will.

TERESA. You're lying to me. The chip shop is open till twelve.

OFFICER. Go to your room.

TERESA. Do I have to, Pat?

PAT. Go to your room.

MISS GILCHRIST. What is going to happen to him, Mr. Pat?

PAT. Go to your room.

MISS GILCHRIST. Oh, Leslie, what's going to become of you?

SOLDIER. I don't know, mum. Maybe I'll be saved at the last minute or maybe I won't.

MISS GILCHRIST. I will give you my prayers.

SOLDIER. Thanks.

MISS GILCHRIST. I will give you a picture.

SOLDIER. Oh, she's nice.

MISS GILCHRIST. Oh, don't you recognize me?

SOLDIER. Oh, it's you, mum.

Enter a shadowy figure with a gun: the OFFICER.

Things might get a bit warm around here; I think you'd better go.

MISS GILCHRIST. God go with you, boy.

She goes off humming.

SOLDIER. Well, that's got rid of her—now the question is will Teresa go to the cops? Or won't she? The place is surrounded and even if Einstein is half sozzled there's the others outside. Will they shoot me? Yes! I suppose so. Would Teresa go to the cops? No!

There is a loud report off stage. The SOLDIER *flings himself on the ground. Sirens, whistles, etc., heard off-stage. Black-out.*

Blimey.

MEG. It's the police! Pat! Pat! Where are you?

PAT. I'm here. Take cover. There's a raid on.

SOLDIER. Where's Teresa?

MEG. Teresa!

PAT. I don't know. She's not here. Get down, get your head down—we're being raided, they'll open fire any minute.

MULLEADY [*up in the flies*]. Two of you stay on the roof. The rest come down through the attic with me.

PRINCESS GRACE. Six at the back and six round the front, two come through the cellar with me.

PAT. And take your partners for the eightsome reel.

MULLEADY. O'Shaunessy, shine a light for Jesus' sake.

O'SHAUNESSY [*off stage*]. I will, sir.

MULLEADY. Shine a light, I can't see a bloody thing.

O'SHAUNESSY [*off stage*]. I can't, sir, the battery's gone.

MULLEADY. To hell with the battery.

PRINCESS GRACE [*off stage*]. Come on, boys, stand by. O.K. there, we're going over.

MULLEADY [*off stage*]. Right, down you go, Shaun.

O'SHAUNESSY [*off stage*]. Will you go first, sir. I'm nervous of the height.

PRINCESS GRACE. Keep your heads down.

MULLEADY. Up de Valera—charge!

PAT. They'll have a job getting through my cellar—with the piano, the parrot and six volumes of the Encyclopaedia.

A flare is lighted. MONSEWER *comes in playing bagpipes.*
Psst. Get your head down.

MONSEWER. What?

PAT. Get your head down!—or we're dead.

MONSEWER. What's happening?

PAT. Hold on and I'll tell you. There's a raid on.

MONSEWER. Why the devil didn't you tell me? What's happening, Patrick?

He goes carefully to the window.

PAT. They're just taking the field, the secret police is ready for the kick off, but the regulars is hanging back—Mr. Mulleady has placed himself at the head of the forces of law and order—and Miss Gilchrist is bringing up his rear. Princess Grace has joined the Police, she's leading a platoon.

MONSEWER. Where's that officer chap?

PAT. He's nowhere to be seen. Disappeared, sir.

MONSEWER. Do you mean to say he's deserted in the face of fire?

PAT. They're coming in.

SOLDIER. Teresa!

MEG. Shut up or I'll plug you and your informer bitch when she comes in.

SOLDIER. Right, mum.

PAT. They're advancing. I think we've had it.

MONSEWER. Up the Republic. Don't fire till you see the whites of their eyes.

MEG. Let's run for it.

MONSEWER. Hold fast!

PAT. I'm running.

MULLEADY. Halt or I fire. Halt!

PAT. I'm halting.

PRINCESS GRACE. Charge!

Guns, machine-guns, smoke.

MONSEWER. Forward! Into the breach! Up the Republic!

SOLDIER. Up Arsenal!

MULLEADY. Hands up! We're coming in.

MONSEWER. If you come in we'll shoot the prisoner.

MEG. Yes.

TERESA [*off*]. Let him go. Leslie, run for it. Leslie, run!

SOLDIER. I'm coming, Teresa.

TERESA. Run!

Shots. SOLDIER *falls.*

MULLEADY AND PRINCESS GRACE. We're coming in.

MONSEWER. Patrick, we're surrounded.

MEG. Put that gun down or I'll kick you up the backside.

PAT, MEG, *and* MONSEWER *put their hands up.*

MONSEWER [*to* MULLEADY]. Who are you?

MULLEADY. I'm a secret policeman and I don't care who knows it. Arrest those women.

The VOLUNTEER *and* OFFICER I.R.A. *enter disguised as women.*

TERESA *runs in.*

TERESA. Where's Leslie?

PAT. He was here a minute ago.

TERESA. Where is he? Leslie!

She sees him.

MEG. There he is.

PAT. He's dead. Take his identification disc.

PRINCESS GRACE [*kneels to do so*]. I did not know he was a Catholic.

TERESA. I gave it him. Leave it with him.

MULLEADY. Cover him up.

TERESA. Leslie—my love—a thousand blessings go with you.

PAT. Don't cry, Teresa—and don't blame anybody for it. Nobody meant to kill him.

TERESA. But he's dead.

PAT. And so is the boy in Belfast Jail.

TERESA. Ah, it was not Belfast Jail or the six counties that was bothering you—but your lost youth and your crippled leg. I will never forget him. He died in a strange land and at home he has no one. I will never forget you, Leslie. Never, till the end of time. [*She turns away.*]

SOLDIER [*sings*].

> The bells of hell
> Go ting-a-ling-a-ling
> For you but not for me.
> Oh death where is thy
> Sting-a-ling-a-ling
> Or grave thy victory?
> If you meet the undertaker
> Or the young man from the Pru,
> Get a pint with what's left over.
> Now I'll say goodbye to you.